Ship of Miracles

14,000 Lives and One Miraculous Voyage

Bill Gilbert

Foreword by Alexander M. Haig Jr.

TRIUMPH
B O O K S
CHICAGO

Library of Congress Cataloging-in-Publication Data

Gilbert, Bill, 1931–
    Ship of miracles: 14,000 lives and one miraculous voyage / Bill Gilbert ;
    foreword by General Alexander M. Haig Jr.
        p. cm.
    ISBN 1-57243-366-3
        1. Korean War, 1950–1953—Search and rescue operations—Korea
    (North)—Hængnam-si. 2. Korean War, 1950–1953—Evacuation of civilians—Korea (North)—Hængnam-si. 3. Korean War, 1950–1953—Naval
    operations, American. 4. Merchant marine—United States—History. I. Title.

DS921.5.S4. G55 2000
951.904'245—dc21

                                                                    00-059383

This book is available in quantity at special discounts for your group or organization. For further information, contact:

Triumph Books
601 South LaSalle Street
Suite 500
Chicago, Illinois 60605
(312) 939-3330
Fax (312) 663-3557

Printed in the United States of America.

ISBN 1-57243-366-3

Book design by Patricia Frey.

Author photograph on back flap copyright © Paul Conway/RoJay Photographers, Rockville, Maryland.

" . . . the greatest rescue operation by a single ship in the history of mankind."

—United States Maritime Administration News Release
August 21, 1960

"Freedom is not free."

—Inscription on the Korean War Veterans Memorial
in Washington, D.C.

To

The Brave and Honorable Men

Of the *Meredith Victory,*

Their Comrades at Hungnam,

And the Refugees They Saved

This Book Is

Gratefully and Respectfully

Dedicated.

Other Books by Bill Gilbert

Over Here, Over There: The Andrews Sisters and the USO Stars in World War II, with Maxene Andrews

They Also Served: Baseball and the Home Front, 1941–1945

How to Talk to Anyone, Anytime, Anywhere, with talk show host Larry King

The Duke of Flatbush, with baseball Hall of Famer Duke Snider

Real Grass, Real Heroes: Baseball's Historic 1941 Season, with baseball All-Star Dom Dimaggio

Now Pitching: Bob Feller, with baseball Hall of Famer Bob Feller

Five O'Clock Lightning, with baseball All-Star Tommy Henrich

The Truth of the Matter, with Bert Lance

This City, This Man: The Cookingham Era in Kansas City

All These Mornings, with *Washington Post* columnist Shirley Povich

Keep Off My Turf, with football All-Pro Mike Curtis

They Call Me the Big E, with basketball Hall of Famer Elvin Hayes

A Coach for All Seasons, with basketball Hall of Famer Morgan Wootten

From Orphans to Champions, with basketball Hall of Famer Morgan Wootten

High School Basketball: How to Be a Winner in Every Way, with coach Joe Gallagher

Municipal Public Relations, with selected authors

The 500 Home Run Club: Baseball's 16 Greatest Home Run Hitters from Babe Ruth to Mark McGwire, with Bob Allen

Contents

Foreword

From One
Who Was There

By Alexander M. Haig Jr.

Fifty years cannot dim the memory of that awful first winter of the Korean War, especially the evacuation of Hungnam—"the forgotten battle in the forgotten war."

As an aide to our commander, Major General Ned Almond, I was an eyewitness to the bravery of America's fighting men and their extraordinary humanitarianism and courage amid extremely heavy combat conditions and the most severe weather imaginable. In the face of rapidly advancing Chinese and North Korean armies in subzero temperatures, units of the United States Army, Navy, Marines, and Merchant Marines fought off the enemy, saved one hundred thousand American young men, and rescued a comparable number of North Korean refugees who were fleeing from their own army and dictatorial government.

This is the story of that memorable time—Christmas 1950—when we were fighting a new war in a far-off land, a hot war in the first years of the Cold War. There was widespread belief that this war, as bad as it was from its very beginning only six months earlier, was also the prelude to a much wider war, one that might well eventually involve the United States and the Soviet Union on opposite sides of the fighting. And if that happened, could World War III be far behind?

I was at Hungnam with General Almond, 135 miles into enemy territory, when the dramatic, lifesaving battles and rescues described in this book took place. I was just beginning my military career and as a young captain I had recently been exposed to combat for the first time. Mere words cannot describe the severity of the conditions, the fury of the fighting, the numbness of the winter, the drama of the withdrawal of our American troops, and the heartbreaking plight of the North Korean refugees.

We got them all, soldiers and refugees, off that beach at Hungnam—our fellow Americans and the North Koreans who were, remember, the men, women, and children of our enemy. That never made any difference to any of us, especially to the gallant men on our Navy and Merchant Marine ships. As they looked at the hard to believe sight of nearly one hundred thousand refugees pleading to be rescued and worked frantically to get them on board and out of harm's way, no one challenged the refugees' nationality or politics or asked for their identification. They were the innocent victims of war. Besides, there was no time for questions. There were lives to be saved.

This book is the story of that miraculous effort, especially by the men of the U.S. Merchant Marine freighter the SS *Meredith Victory*. Every American who fought at Hungnam to protect the rescuers and the refugees, and those who helped to save two hundred thousand American and Korean lives, can take pride in this story.

Korea remains divided today. The war technically goes on, quiet only because of a truce signed in 1953. Despite recent signs of hope, the story of Hungnam and the *Meredith Victory* also goes on, a brilliant yet relatively unknown chapter in American history that can now take its place, during this fiftieth anniversary of the Korean War, among such other legendary names as Bunker Hill, Midway, the Battle of the Bulge, Iwo Jima, and Okinawa.

This book did not just deserve to be written—it *needed* to be written. I am proud to have been a part of what happened at Hungnam. Fifty years later, I am proud to be a part of the telling of that heroic story.

Editor's note: Alexander Haig later became White House chief of staff under President Richard Nixon, commander of the North Atlantic Treaty Organization (NATO), and secretary of state under President Ronald Reagan.

Roll Call

Many men and women helped me to tell this story by providing information, photographs, and valuable suggestions. All of them have my gratitude, especially Colonel Charles P. Borchini, chief of commemorations for the Fiftieth Anniversary of the Korean War Commemoration Committee, and his entire professional staff, particularly Major Bob White, Major Peter Kemp, Technical Sergeant Valerie Phelps, and Gina Di Nicolo.

Others who deserve a special place in this roll call include:

Sherwood (Woody) Goldberg, senior adviser to General Alexander M. Haig Jr.

Father Joel, Abbot of Saint Paul's Abbey, Newton, New Jersey

Father Anton Kang, director of the Benedictine Research Center, Seoul, South Korea

The staff of the United States Maritime Administration, especially Doris Turner and Pat Thomas

Fred Carrier and Julie Park of the Korea Society

Tom Maines of the Society of the Third Infantry Division

Peter Kim and Michael Inglis, assistants to the Reverend Sun Myung Moon

Larry Moffitt, vice president of *The Washington Times* Foundation

William J. Davis, executive director of the General Douglas MacArthur Foundation

Colonel Warren Wiedham, president and chief executive officer of the U.S.-Korea 2000 Foundation, Inc.

Alexander Mansourov of the Brookings Institution

Author Link White

The publishing team at Triumph Books of Chicago, starting at the top with publisher Mitch Rogatz and including, in alphabetical order, Kris Anstrats, Olivia Satenberg, Blythe Smith, and Karyn Viverito.

Prominent mention is reserved for Dr. Jean Mansavage, the historian for Colonel Borchini's staff in 1999, who made it possible for others to learn this story fifty years later by calling it to my attention, and who then provided the highest level of professional assistance. Without her, the current and future generations would never know the heroic and humanitarian story of the SS *Meredith Victory*.

Acknowledgments

Acknowledgment is gratefully made to the following sources for permission to quote passages from their publications:

Penguin Putnam, Inc., for the use of *Plain Speaking: An Oral Biography of Harry S. Truman* by Merle Miller, copyright © 1973 by Merle Miller. Used by permission of Putnam Berkley, a division of Penguin Putnam, Inc.

Facts on File, for the use of the *Korean War Almanac*, by Harry G. Summers Jr., © 1990.

U.S. News & World Report, for the use of their cover story of June 25, 1990: "40 Years After Korea—The Forgotten War," copyright © June 25, 1990, *U.S. News and World Report*.

Dr. Kim Hakjoon, president of the University of Inchon, for the use of his paper "Russian Foreign Ministry Documents on the Origins of the Korean War." Presented at The Korean War: An Assessment of the Historical Record, a conference held at Georgetown University, Washington, D.C., July 24–25, 1995, and sponsored by the Korea Society, Korea-America Society, and Georgetown University.

Dr. Evgueni Bajanov, director of the Institute for Contemporary International Problems, Russian Foreign Ministry, Moscow, for the use of his paper "Assessing the Politics of the Korean War." Presented at The Korean War: An Assessment of the Historical Record, a conference held at Georgetown University, Washington, D.C., July 24–25, 1995, and sponsored by the Korea Society, Korea-America Society, and Georgetown University.

The General Douglas MacArthur Memorial Foundation, for the use of "Christmas Cargo: A Civilian Account of the Hungnam Evacuation," by Dr. Bong Hak Hyun, M.D., D.Sc., as told to Marian Hyun; and for the use of "M*A*S*H: The Last Days (December 1950) at Hungnam, North Korea, with the First Mobile Army Surgical Hospital," by Lieutenant Colonel Carl T. Dubuy, Medical Corps, United States Army. Both articles were published in the foundation's *Korean War Special*, © 1997.

Presidio Press, for the use of *America's Tenth Legion* by Shelby L. Stanton. Available from Presidio Press, Novato, California.

Naval Institute Press, for the use of *Colder Than Hell* by Joseph R. Owen, © 1999.

Map of the Korean Peninsula

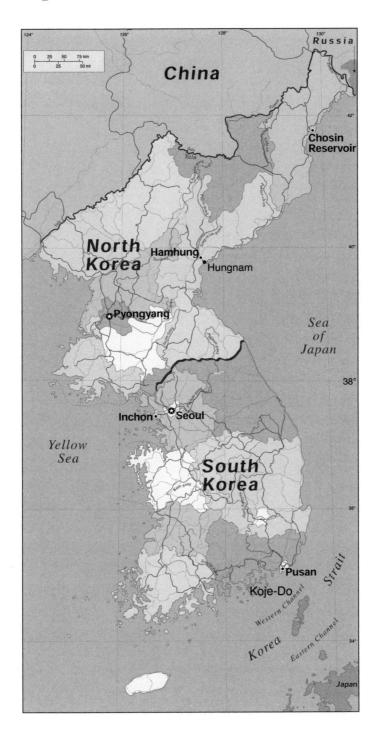

Introduction

A Salute

Millions of Americans in their sixties and older remember the escape of one hundred thousand American troops from North Korea and their evacuation from the port city of Hungnam in the sixth month of the new Korean War, Christmastime 1950. As one who served in the United States Air Force for two and a half years of that war and for another eighteen months after the shooting stopped, I remember it vividly.

As brave as the American fighting men were, their courage was matched by the men on the ships in the harbor who were working against time to save virtually the same number of North Korean refugees. This book tells that other, lesser-known story.

Books have been written about the breakout of the American soldiers and Marines from the Chosin Reservoir in mid-December of that year and of their struggle to reach Hungnam, where ships waited to evacuate them. The other story that was unfolding at the same time, the rescue of the North Korean refugees—especially the gallant role of the *Meredith Victory*—has been largely overlooked. At the time of the dramatic breakout at Chosin, the attention of most Americans was on our own fighting men and not on the North Korean people and the life-or-death dangers confronting them.

Articles about the refugees and the victorious efforts by the Americans to save them appeared occasionally in the 1950s and '60s when the men of the *Meredith Victory* received recognition from the United States government and from the government of South Korea. But that was forty years ago. Few Americans have ever known the story of the *Meredith Victory*, even during the days immediately following the evacuation of Hungnam. Today, virtually no one has heard this story.

Those who served in the American armed forces during the Korean War, especially those who faced combat, have always deserved better treatment than they have received from the history books. Long before the Vietnam veterans began complaining, with reason, that they were being neglected, the veterans of the war before theirs, Korea, experienced the same forgotten feeling. The oversight continues to this day, when reporters and news anchors cover Memorial Day and Veterans' Day ceremonies with words and pictures honoring the men and women of World War II and Vietnam while frequently not mentioning even one word about the Korean War.

This book is an attempt to tell the story of the human drama of Hungnam and the *Meredith Victory* in the full context of the war—the conditions and miscalculations that caused it, the bravery of the refugees themselves in the terror, uncertainty, and overpowering conditions that surrounded them, and the atmosphere in the United States, back on "the home front."

But the book is more than that. It is also a salute to the heroes of Hungnam—the American fighting men who kept the charging enemy off the beach so the evacuation could succeed and the men on the ships in the harbor who helped the refugees to scramble on board and then endured the weather, the mines in the water, and threats from the enemy to sail to safety with their human cargo.

It is this author's hope that, in the process of recording this story for history and rendering this salute to our forces who were at Hungnam, I have also helped to make the American people aware of "America's forgotten war"—and to make us grateful to the men and women who were there.

—Bill Gilbert, Washington, D.C., June 2000

Chapter One

Innocent Victims and Their Terror

In bone-chilling temperatures and howling winds, with the imminent threat of enemy gunfire aimed at his ship from the beach and return fire from the USS *Missouri,* four destroyers, two heavy cruisers, and four rocket ships sailing over him back toward the shore, destiny was summoning a thirty-seven-year-old Merchant Marine captain from Philadelphia.

Captain Leonard LaRue stood on the deck of his five-year-old, ten-thousand-ton freighter, the SS *Meredith Victory,* in the harbor at Hungnam, North Korea, 135 miles into enemy territory, in the sixth month of the Korean War, Christmastime 1950. "I trained my binoculars on the shore and saw a pitiable scene," he later wrote. "Korean refugees thronged the docks. With them was everything they could wheel, carry, or drag. Beside them, like frightened chicks, were their children."

He was looking at nearly one hundred thousand terrified North Korean refugees—old men, women of every age, and children, the innocent victims of every war—who were desperately fleeing the Chinese Communists, who had threatened to behead any North Korean civilians, even though they were supposedly on the same side. The Chinese angrily charged that the civilians had been aiding the Americans and their allies.

Hundreds, even thousands, of family tragedies were unfolding on those docks. Kim Jung Hee, a twenty-nine-year-old mother of three young children—two daughters and a son—carried her youngest child, Won Suk, a little girl about two years old, on her back. At the same time she clutched the hand of her son, five-year-old Doo Hyuk, with one hand and held her husband's hand with the other as he carried their oldest child, their ten-year-old daughter, Koon Ja.

They lived in the North Korean city of Wonsan, sixty miles south of Hungnam. They owned a jewelry store where they sold diamonds and other gems. As the war grew worse, and with their fear of the Communist regime in the north, they made the fateful decision to leave Wonsan and escape to South Korea, where they hoped to find safety and freedom for themselves and their children.

They were so desperate that they were willing to walk, even in the subzero temperatures and with snow on the ground. Kim Jung Hee's nephew, Major Peter Kemp, is now a major in the United States Army. He relayed questions from me to his aunt, who is now seventy-nine years old and lives in Seoul. Together we were able to piece together her story.

They left her husband's parents behind in Wonsan. Her husband's brothers and sisters had already been drafted into the North Korean Army. Kim Jung Hee's own family lived much farther away, near the border of Siberia, so she was forced to leave them behind, too. Their decision to leave their families was made easier, she said, because everyone believed that those who were evacuating would be able to return to their homes in only a few months. The rumor going around was that the United Nations forces were retreating, but that their retreat was only temporary—everyone would soon be able to come back home. Neither Kim Jung Hee nor her husband, Lee Man Sik, ever saw their parents or other family members again.

The walk "seemed like forever," Kim Jung Hee recalled. It was "very cloudy," she said, and "extremely cold." She estimated that their journey took at least two days, maybe several more. As they walked, they passed the bodies of those who were not able to survive even the first leg of their desperate journey to safety and freedom. There were "a lot" of people on the road, also traveling by foot to Hungnam, lending credibility to statements by veterans of Hungnam that the North Korean people "were voting with their feet," expressing their displeasure over the ironfisted rule of the Communist Party in their country.

On the way to Hungnam they were strafed and bombed by war planes. Kim Jung Hee was unable to tell whether they were American or Russian planes. They had to dive for cover on the side of the road several times. The parents almost became separated from their children during the air attacks when all of them ran for protection from the planes as they swooped down on the wide-open refugees.

After they reached Hungnam, they found that the scene at the city's dock was "chaotic," with pushing and shoving and soldiers trying to separate the refugees from military personnel so the refugees wouldn't board the ships intended to transport the troops. After the military boarding was complete, the soldiers still on the beach (the men of the United States Army's Third Infantry Division) helped the refugees to board other ships to sail out of the harbor at Hungnam and head for the southern tip of Korea and another port city, Pusan.

As the vast crowd surged back and forth, with refugees extending all the way to the horizon and more flooding in by the minute, Kim Jung Hee's husband told her he was going to look for food for the family. Lee Man Sik took their daughter Koon Ja with him. He told his wife, "Stand here. We'll be right back." After he left, the throng grew more desperate due to both the sheer numbers and the growing fear among the refugees that the American ships might leave at any minute. The refugees were urging those in front of them to hurry, to board the ship—not knowing what kind it was, where it was headed, or what their fate might be if they boarded it. All they knew was that it was a ship, and a ship—any kind—was their only hope for survival.

Kim Jung Hee felt the surge of the crowd around her and heard people telling her to keep moving ahead. She wanted to wait right there, as her husband had told her. She was afraid that any step in any direction would mean they would not find each other. But even her neighbors from Wonsan around her were growing anxious. As the eagerness of everyone on the dock increased, the force of the crowd pushed the young mother and her two children toward a ship, an American "LST" (the Navy's initials for landing ships that carry tanks). Some in the mass of humanity were telling her, "Come on. Let's go. This may be the last ship out."

Those who saw the scene at Hungnam in 1950 say that it was like that other famous scene of desperate human beings, the people of South Vietnam who overran the United States embassy in Saigon and reached for the helicopters from the roof as American personnel completed their pullout at the end of the war in 1975.

At Hungnam, the crowd literally pushed Kim Jung Hee on board the LST with her two children. As she looked around anxiously but futilely for her husband and their third child, she never imagined in her worst fears that she would spend the rest of her life looking for them. Today, as she enters her eighties, she still looks.

*   *   *   *   *

A seventeen-year-old schoolgirl, Jung Park, stood with her mother, hoping against hope to be squeezed onto one of the countless fishing boats that bobbed up and down in the harbor.

By the time Jung and the rest of the jam-packed passengers sailed out of Hungnam in their small boat, the ship rode only inches above the water. Eventually the refugees were forced to throw all of their earthly possessions overboard, those few belongings they had been able to pack on their backs or on ox-drawn carts to the beach. Jung painfully threw over her brother's accordion and guitar, two of her family's few sources of happiness during the five years of harsh Communist dictatorship in North Korea since the end of World War II.

Another schoolgirl, Soon Park (no relation to Jung), was hurriedly transported by pickup truck from her school in Hamhung, only eight miles away, after her teacher urged the family to leave immediately for Hungnam and try to get on a boat.

Soon's grandfather was the first Christian minister in North Korea and her family was strongly anti-Communist. Word had reached Hamhung that her family was in danger and should evacuate. School officials provided a truck and offered to drive the family to Hungnam with other students, but Soon's mother refused. Instead, crying and frantic, she chose to stay home to be with Soon's father, employed by a construction company, and their only son. Meanwhile Soon, separated from her family, began the drive toward Hungnam with her classmates, on roads already crowded with other fleeing refugees. It was the first time she had ever left home.

Soon, now retired after working as an instructor and an office clerk in a driving school that she owned with her husband in Kensington, Maryland, remembers that the students all expected to return to Hamhung "in three days." She was unable to return, and never saw her parents again.

Other refugees suffered similar trials. Ashley Halsey Jr. described some of them less than four months later in *The Saturday Evening Post* of April 14, 1951: "One man brought only his violin. A woman struggled across the gangway with her sewing machine on her head. An entire family began shoving a piano aboard, until told the space was needed for people. Soon people filled every space below decks. Some sat cross-legged and crammed together. Latecomers stood like bus or subway riders during the rush hour. A three-year-old girl held a live chicken in her hand."

The officers and crew on the *Meredith Victory* watched the scene in horrified disbelief from offshore, with no way of knowing that fate was about to tap them for the most historic role of any of the 193 Navy warships, Merchant Marine freighters, and tiny fishing boats crowding Hungnam's harbor. The ship and her crew were, in fact, about to set a new standard for heroism in naval combat.

The scene of desperation and panic against the backdrop of booming modern warfare was a climactic moment in the largest and most dramatic sea rescue operation in history, a miraculous accomplishment that has been compared to the escape of 350,000 Allied soldiers from the charging Nazis on the beach at Dunkirk, France, ten years earlier.

Barely six thousand yards away, in hot pursuit as they approached a defense perimeter manned by United States soldiers, were 120,000 North Korean and Chinese Communist soldiers ordered to kill the refugees or capture them as prisoners. In front of the refugees was the vastness of the Sea of Japan, their only hope for escape to the safety and freedom of Pusan on the southern tip of South Korea.

The situation at Hungnam's harbor was the latest flash point in the world's newest war, one whose first six months had been marked by a roller-coaster ride of crises and triumphs, of shocking turns, a war that in itself surprised most Americans, many of whom didn't even know where Korea was.

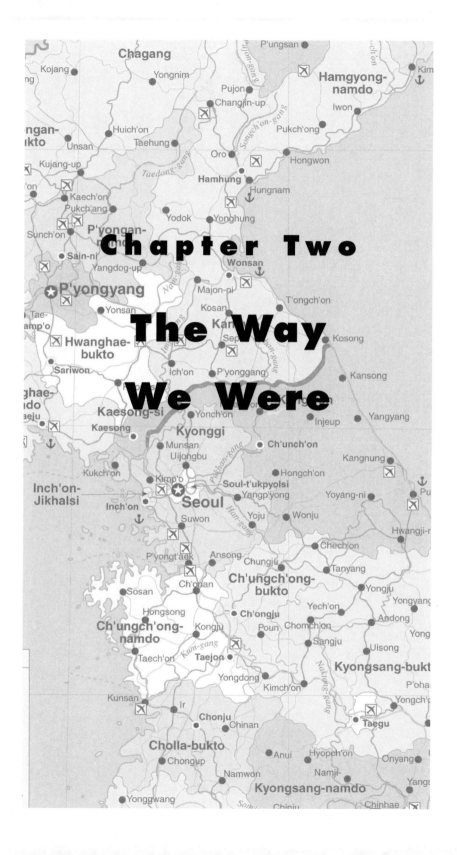

Chapter Two
The Way
We Were

Korea was governed by Japan until Japan's surrender in 1945 at the end of World War II. The two new super powers in what became the Cold War, the United States and the Soviet Union, strongly disagreed about what Korea's fate should be. The Americans called for free elections. The Soviets, under Joseph Stalin, had designs on the peninsula and refused to permit free elections. A compromise was reached when the two nations agreed to split Korea into North and South along the 38th parallel.

On May 10, 1948, free elections were held in South Korea under United Nations supervision; there were no elections in North Korea. The Republic of Korea—South Korea—was established, with its capital in Seoul, under President Syngman Rhee, a strong-willed seventy-three-year-old who had long pushed for a free Korea. In the North, the Democratic People's Republic of Korea was established, with its capital in Pyongyang. The government was headed by thirty-six-year-old Kim Il Sung, a much younger man than Rhee.

On March 23, 1949, President Truman approved the withdrawal of all United States troops from South Korea except for five hundred members of a Korean military advisory group. One year later to the month, on March 10, 1950, twenty-nine guerrilla attacks took place in South Korea, as well as eighteen incidents along the 38th parallel. In May the number of attacks and incidents dropped sharply.

As Americans enjoyed the first heady years of peace in the second half of the 1940s and the first days of the '50s, the two Koreas were experiencing increased tensions. Whatever concern Americans felt at that time about international tensions, however, stemmed not from Asia but from Europe, where Stalin was threatening hostilities over the divided city of Berlin, blockading the city in June of 1948 in an attempt to force the Allies out by starving the 2.5 million German residents into submission.

After President Truman ordered the Berlin Airlift and the Soviets backed down in September of 1949, Americans paid little attention to events in Asia, certainly not some place with the strange name of Korea. Instead, they were enjoying life. Their love affair with the automobile reached something of a new level with the manufacture of more than 5 million new automobiles. They were flocking to the movies to see *All The King's Men* with Broderick Crawford and *Adam's Rib* starring Spencer Tracy and Katharine Hepburn. On Broadway they were enjoying *South Pacific* with Mary Martin and Ezio Pinza, *Death of a Salesman* with Lee J. Cobb, and *Gentlemen Prefer Blondes*, starring Carol Channing.

Movies were still a favorite entertainment for Americans, but something else was giving them pleasure, too. We were going wild over our newest source of amusement, television. We sat fascinated in our living rooms with the lights out and watched shows like *Stop the Music*, hosted by Bert Parks, *The Life of Riley*, starring William Bendix, and *Mama,* with Peggy Wood. Our viewing habits were changing, and so were our living habits. Our routines were being influenced by a new question sure to be heard every day: "What's on TV tonight?" And schoolchildren were being told something new: "No TV until you've finished your homework."

We were singing the hit songs of the day—"Dear Hearts and Gentle People," "Mule Train," "Some Enchanted Evening," and

Gene Autry's new Christmas favorite, "Rudolph The Red-Nosed Reindeer." The New York Yankees were winning the first of their five straight World Series championships under their new manager, Casey Stengel, over the annual sentimental favorites, the Brooklyn Dodgers.

Even the serious business of attempting to achieve a lasting peace was a cause for optimism. After John D. Rockefeller contributed several million dollars, the cornerstone was laid for the headquarters of the United Nations on the banks of the East River in New York. Yet as 1949 turned into 1950 and Americans began to hear and read about the greatest this and the greatest that of the first half of the twentieth century, developments began unfolding that threatened what peace we had in those first years of the Cold War.

Secretary of State Dean Acheson mysteriously sent the wrong signal to the Kremlin with a speech at the National Press Club in Washington in January of 1950. Acheson declared that Korea was outside the perimeter of America's vital interests, a statement that could have understandably been interpreted by Stalin in Moscow and Kim Il Sung in Pyongyang as an indication that America would not get involved in defending South Korea in the event of hostilities that might be started by the North.

A young Army lieutenant, newly married and stationed in Tokyo on the staff of General Douglas MacArthur, remembers Acheson's statement to this day. Alexander M. Haig was destined to become White House chief of staff under President Nixon, a four-star general, commander of the North Atlantic Treaty Organization (NATO), and secretary of state under President Reagan. In April 2000 his memory of Acheson's speech and MacArthur's reaction to it was still clear.

"I can remember how upset MacArthur was," he told me. "I worked right there in his chief's office. That meant I saw him every day. I'd bring papers in to him frequently. I got to know him quite well. He was infuriated at that statement."

When I asked General Haig why Acheson would say such a thing, knowing it was an open invitation to Stalin to go ahead and start something in Korea, Haig said, "I think he genuinely believed it"—that Korea was not a concern of ours.

Did he do it on his own, or did he clear the statement with President Truman before he made it?

"Nobody knows."

Haig added, as one secretary of state evaluating another, "Acheson in other respects was a brilliant guy, far better than he ever got credit for. He was a European expert, totally oriented toward Europe. That dominated the initial phase of the war because the great fear in Washington and the State Department was that by standing up in South Korea—can you believe it?—Berlin would be overrun. That was the main inhibitor, and that's why we sat there with both arms tied behind our backs. It was just bad, bad thinking."

Acheson was not the first American official, or team of officials, to express a distinct lack of enthusiasm for rushing to South Korea's military aid in the event of war. In September 1947 America's military leaders, the Joint Chiefs of Staff, said that "from the standpoint of military security, the United States has little strategic interest in maintaining the present troops and bases in Korea."

Generals Dwight Eisenhower and Carl Spaatz and Admirals William Leahy and Chester Nimitz said our forty-five thousand troops in Korea "would be a liability." By the time General Omar Bradley succeeded Eisenhower in 1948 as the Army chief of staff, United States troop strength in South Korea had been reduced to thirty thousand. The last of their number were withdrawn on June 29, 1949, six months after the last Soviet troops left.

In the same month of the report by the Joint Chiefs, Truman authorized work to proceed with the development of the world's first hydrogen bomb, which was detonated one year and four months later. The military draft was extended for another year. Senator Joseph McCarthy, a Republican from Wisconsin, made headlines during a speech by holding up what he said was a list of more than two hundred communists who were working in the Department of State. Shortly after, editorial cartoonist Herb Block ("Herblock") of *The Washington Post* coined a new term: McCarthyism.

In 1950, the people of South Korea were enjoying their first years of freedom despite repeated threats from North Korea. Above the 38th parallel, however, people were not nearly so happy. Grim assessments of life in that nation came later from twelve North Koreans who were evacuated from Hungnam and settled in South Korea after the war. They were interviewed by members of the Eighth Army in a follow-up report released in December 1975, twenty-five years after the start of the war.

Stanley F. Bolin, who was then the chief of the United States Army Research Unit in Korea, wrote, "When asked to recall what, if anything, had made them happy during the period between the Japanese surrender and their own evacuation in 1950, most answered, 'Nothing.' The few who had been financially well-off commented that even their relative affluence had brought little joy in the face of political pressure under the Northern regime."

The Bolin report continued, "Several recalled with distaste the plundering of their homes by Russian soldiers around the time of the Japanese surrender. In later years some had had their land confiscated and their businesses taxed almost out of existence by the Communist government. Others had lived under constant surveillance by the authorities. One man lost both of his parents and two younger brothers as the Communists set out to exterminate political opposition. During the time frame the individual aspirations of those interviewed had ranged from a type of dismal hopelessness to a dream of national unification under a non-oppressive government."

*   *   *   *   *

Just before dawn on Sunday, June 25, 1950, as South Koreans tasted freedom for the first time, rain, some of it heavy, began to fall along the border between North and South Korea. Units of the North Korean Army, suddenly and without warning after the lull in May, attacked South Korea across the entire 38th parallel, from the west to the east. Their first invasion of South Korean territory was on the Ongjin Peninsula at 4:00 A.M. At 11:00 A.M, the North Korean government announced that North Korea had declared war on South Korea.

In an eerie case of history repeating itself, many of the officers and men of the South Korean Army were away from their posts on weekend passes at the time of the attacks, just as American soldiers and sailors at Pearl Harbor had been enjoying their weekend nine years earlier when they, too, became the victims of a sneak attack.

In Seoul the day was dawning with an overcast sky and a light rain. Heavy rain was predicted for the coming weeks. The phone rang on the Command Group duty officer's desk at the headquarters of the Supreme Commander for the Allied Powers (SCAP)—General Douglas MacArthur—in downtown Tokyo. It was just before dawn. The duty officer, Lieutenant Haig, answered.

From the other end of the phone, the American ambassador to Seoul, John J. Muccio, spoke through a scratchy, static-filled connection and alerted Haig that large numbers of North Korean troops had crossed the 38th parallel at around 4:00 A.M. and were attacking South Korean troops and installations—shattering the predawn quiet in a nation whose name means "land of the morning calm."

Haig thus became the first military officer in Tokyo to learn that the Korean War had started. In his 1992 autobiography *Inner Circles* with Charles McCarry he wrote that American intelligence sources had warned "no fewer than fifteen hundred times since June 1949" that a Communist invasion from North Korea into the South was imminent. To make it clear that this was the real McCoy, the ambassador emphasized to the young officer, "Lieutenant, this is not a false alarm."

Haig answered, "Understood, Mr. Ambassador. Your message will be passed to SCAP immediately."

Haig promptly called MacArthur's chief of staff, Major General Edward M. Almond—Ned—and reported the grim and alarming news. Haig was an aide-de-camp to Almond. When Almond expressed understandable skepticism after so many similar reports in the past year, Haig stressed, "Sir, the ambassador said, 'This is not a false alarm.'"

Almond called MacArthur, who said, "Very well, Ned. Assemble the staff and prepare your recommendations. I will be in at seven o'clock."

The American role in the Korean War was beginning.

Back home, the shock was immediate and profound. If many members of the general public did not know much about Korea, where it was, or why it was important to the United States, the nation's newspaper editors did. The reaction of *The Washington Star* was typical. It ran an eight-column banner line, across the top of its front page:

REDS INVADE SOUTH KOREA ON WIDE FRONT

Below the banner line was an Associated Press report:

> SEOUL, Sunday, June 25—Communist troops from North Korea invaded South Korea at dawn today on a wide front, but American military advisers said the invasion was virtually stopped by this afternoon.

One of the morning papers in the nation's capital, *The Washington Post,* reminded its readers in a lengthy editorial that North Korea was "a Muscovite creature" that "would not move without orders from the Kremlin." The *Post* voiced an ominous warning, pointing to "the danger to world peace in this explosive situation." The paper called for "prompt assistance."

The start of the Korean War was not the top story that morning in either the *Post* or *The New York Times.* Both papers instead led with a report from Milwaukee of a Northwest Air Lines plane that vanished somewhere over Lake Michigan with fifty-eight people on board, all feared to be dead. A second front-page story reported that the French National Assembly had voted Premier Georges Bidault out of office.

The *Times* headline on the war story was blunt:

WAR IS DECLARED BY NORTH KOREANS;
FIGHTING ON BORDER

The paper carried stories from both wire services, which verified the contention by the *Post* that the decision to start the war was made in the Kremlin and not in North Korea. One dispatch said,

"The State Department in Washington, receiving reports of the Korean fighting, was preparing to hold the Soviet Union responsible for the outbreak. The Associated Press quoted Korean ambassador John Myun Chang as saying the North Korean attack was an aggressive action that could not have been carried out 'without Soviet direction . . .'"

The *Star*'s headline the next day was just as frightening as the day before:

REDS REACH SEOUL AND DEMAND SURRENDER

Below were eight page-one stories about the new war.

*　　*　　*　　*　　*

In 1950 Karl Park was a high school senior in North Korea, twenty miles from Pyongyang. "We did not know a war was going to start," he said at the Maryland flower shop he operates with his wife, Jung, the refugee who was forced to throw her brother's guitar and accordion overboard. "But we were not surprised. All the time since 1945 we had been told that Korea would have to be united, because South Korea was a puppet of the United States. This is what the Communists told us."

One of the early indications that war was inevitable, Park remembered, was that by 1949 all high school students were required to belong to the Communist Youth Association. "They intensified our military training," he said, "and talked about Communism— every day and every night. So almost everybody between seventeen and nineteen years old was ready—spiritually and mentally ready. Girls too. They also received military training and regimentation. Plus propaganda. They wanted to make the kids good Communists. So by 1950, we were ready to fight."

Park remembers more disturbing signs early that year. "I noticed equipment and supplies headed south in early February," he said. "Tanks, gasoline in drums—headed toward the 38th parallel."

Park said high school students had three career choices under the Communist government: the army, teaching, or working in the graphite, magnesium, or tungsten mines. He chose to become a teacher even though he knew there would be pressure on him once the North Korean Army achieved complete victory by occupying all of South Korea.

"When that happens," Park said, "we would become Communist agents in South Korea, as organizers in Communist cells working for the party." Only two years ago, Park found out that at that time he had been scheduled to be shipped south as one of the first of those Communist organizers, whether he wanted to go or not.

The bulletin about the start of the war that Park heard in North Korea was exactly the opposite of the truth. The reports in the North were that South Korea had invaded North Korea.

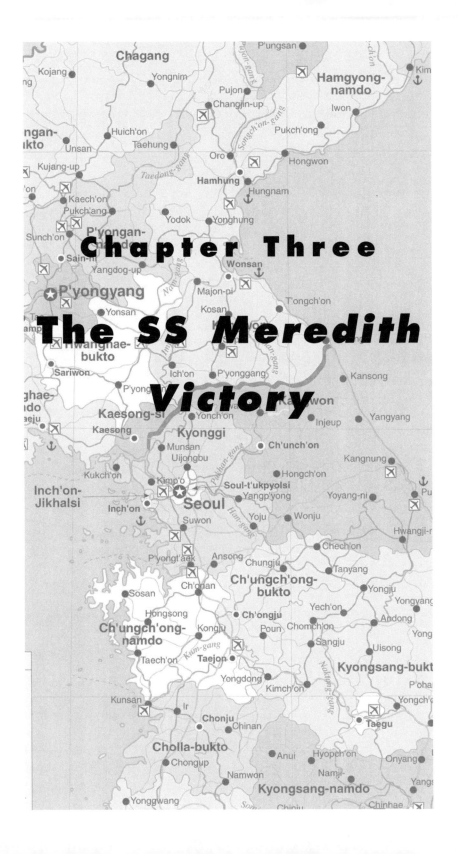

Chapter Three

The SS Meredith Victory

Documents from the Russian Foreign Ministry, turned over to South Korea in 1994 after the collapse of the Soviet Union, create the impression that the war in Korea should not have surprised anyone. Stalin, despite his own concerns that the Americans might react militarily, was anxious to communize South Korea and create one unified nation under Communist—and Soviet—rule. Kim Il Sung likewise wanted to take over the South. Rhee, despite his advanced age, had been agitating for years to take over the North, by military force if necessary. And newly communized "Red China," under Mao Tse Tung, was indicating it would support the military takeover of South Korea.

Dr. Kim Hakjoon, then chair of the Board of Trustees at Dankook University in Seoul and now president of the University of Inchon, told a conference in Washington in 1995 that phone calls and visits to Moscow, Pyongyang, and Beijing, as well as other forms of communication by various leaders of the Soviet Union, North Korea, and Red China, combine to offer an ample body of evidence about Communist plans for a war with South Korea. "Simply put," he wrote in a paper for the conference, "it is wrong to say that the Korean War began on June 25, 1950." In his paper, Dr. Kim quotes Kim Il Sung as saying on January 17, 1950, "Now that the unification of China has been completed, it is our turn to liberate South Korea."

Dr. Kim presented his paper to "The Korean War: An Assessment of the Historical Record," a conference sponsored by the Korea Society, Korea-America Society, and Georgetown University. In his paper, Dr. Kim referred to Acheson's speech, saying, " . . . many people got the impression that the U.S. had abandoned the mission of defending South Korea. Stalin also appears to have gotten that impression." Leaders in Pyongyang, Moscow, and Beijing also believed that the United States would not risk a third world war over a small nation like South Korea.

In his conclusion to the symposium in Washington, Dr. Kim wrote, "However, one thing is crystal clear. The Korean War of 1950–1953 was initiated by Kim Il Sung of North Korea, who regarded the war as a tool for the 'liberation' of South Korea and the ultimate unification of the Korean nation in communist terms. He was sure of his success. As an initiator, Kim persistently attempted to persuade Stalin primarily and Mao secondarily. Kim finally succeeded in doing so. Then the role of Stalin became important. Around March of 1950 Stalin helped Kim in his planning for war, under the premise that Kim would win the war so quickly that the United States could not intervene, even if it wanted to do so. In this sense, Stalin was a facilitator of Kim's plan."

A paper written by another expert at the same symposium, Dr. Evgueni Bajanov, director of the Institute for Contemporary International Problems in the Russian Foreign Ministry in Moscow, makes new revelations about Stalin's involvement. Among his sources, Dr. Bajanov cites "the recently declassified Soviet archives." From his research into those archives, he declares, "Up to the end of 1949, Stalin did not plan any aggression against South Korea. Instead, he was worried about an attack from the South, and did everything to avoid provoking Washington and Seoul. In 1947–1948, Soviet leaders still believed in the possibility of a unification of Korea, and refused to sign a separate friendship and cooperation treaty with Kim Il Sung."

Dr. Bajanov reveals that Stalin was worried about an attack by South Korea in 1948 and 1949. "On April 17, 1949," Dr. Bajanov wrote, "Stalin warned his ambassador of an imminent attack from the South. The Soviet ambassador confirmed that a large-scale war was being prepared by Seoul with the help of Americans and raised alarm about the inability of North Korean troops to withstand the aggression . . . The USSR was clearly afraid of such an attack and was nervous not knowing how to prevent the war. Stalin repeatedly castigated Ambassador Shtykov [Colonel-General Terentiy Shtykov] for failing to do everything in his power to maintain peace on the 38th parallel."

Stalin's position was that the North could attack the South only as a counterattack if the South attacked first. "Then," Stalin told Kim Il Sung in Moscow on March 7, 1949, "your move will be understood and supported by everyone."

Pressure by North Korea for support from the Soviet Union to attack South Korea continued through the balance of 1949. Stalin relented to a degree on September 11, instructing his embassy staff in Pyongyang to assess all aspects of the possible effects of an attack against South Korea. Two weeks later, the Politburo in Moscow warned that such an attack "would give the Americans a pretext for all kinds of interference into Korean affairs."

As 1950 began, Kim Il Sung complained to Soviet Ambassador Shtykov, "I can't sleep at night because I am thinking of the unification of the whole country. If the cause . . . is postponed, then I may lose the confidence of the Korean people."

Ambassador Shtykov relayed Sung's concerns to Moscow. On January 30, Stalin responded through diplomatic channels:

> I understand the unhappiness of comrade Kim Il Sung,
> but he must understand that such a big thing regarding

> South Korea . . . requires thorough preparation. It has
> to be organized in such a way that there will not be a
> large risk. If he wants to talk to me on this issue, then
> I'll always be ready to receive him and talk to him . . .
> I am prepared to help him in this matter.

According to Dr. Bajanov, Stalin changed his mind and decided
to support an attack against South Korea for four reasons: (1) the
Communists had taken over China; (2) the Soviets now had the
atomic bomb, after exploding their first in 1949; (3) the establishment of the North Atlantic Treaty Organization in Europe and
an accompanying increase in East-West tensions had angered
Stalin; and (4) Stalin perceived a "weakening of Washington's
positions and of its will to get involved militarily in Asia."

Dr. Bajanov declares, "Stalin was now more confident of the
Communist bloc's strength, less respectful of American capabil-
ities, and less interested in the reaction of Western public opinion to Communist moves."

*   *   *   *   *

Until the United States and other nations intervened under the
flag of the United Nations, the war was a mismatch. North
Korea, with 150,000 troops under arms, invaded with a fighting
force of 90,000 troops plus 150 Soviet-made tanks, heavy
artillery, and at least fifty Russian Yak fighter planes. The troops
were far from green, inexperienced kids. They were experienced veterans who had fought in World War II. Some had
fought with the Chinese Communists and others had served in
combat for the Soviet Union.

In General Haig's book, he emphatically declares that the
North Korean Army "was equipped with Soviet tanks and

Soviet guns, advised by Soviet officers, and set in motion for Soviet purposes."

In stark contrast, South Korea's fighting force, even in the face of all the threats of the previous year, still consisted of fewer than one hundred thousand men, none of them with combat experience—and no combat airplanes, virtually no artillery, and only enough ammunition to last for several days.

The size and strength of the American military also left something to be desired. General Bradley later wrote that the American demobilization that followed World War II, accompanied by a drastically reduced defense budget, had slashed the Army to a "shockingly deplorable state." He said bluntly that the Army at that point "could not fight its way out of a paper bag." Another senior officer, Lieutenant General Hobart R. Gay, who commanded the First Cavalry Division in Korea, called the Army's lack of combat readiness an "utter disgrace."

Clay Blair, an author and military correspondent, wrote relatively the same thing. In his 1987 book *The Forgotten War* he charges, "For various reasons, it [the Army] was not prepared mentally, physically, or otherwise for war. On the whole, its leadership at the Army, corps, division, regiment, and battalion levels was average, inexperienced, often incompetent, and not physically capable of coping with the rigorous climate of Korea."

Reporter Bill Lawrence of *The New York Times* covered the war in Korea in its early stages, joined by Edward R. Murrow of CBS, both covering their second war involving the United States in five years. Lawrence, who later covered the White House for the *Times*, wrote in his autobiography, *Six Presidents, Too Many Wars,* "The battle in Korea was one for which the United States was ill prepared. The five peacetime years of drastic cutbacks in military expenditures at home, plus some cockeyed ideas of economy-minded Secretaries of Defense, had given us an army so under-equipped and so badly organized that the troops lacked the power to fight well." He added that five years of occupation duty in Japan had hardly conditioned them for combat. "Occupation troops," he said, "are better trained for hand-to-hand combat with geisha girls."

British author and historian Max Hastings also offered evidence of South Korea's dangerous lack of preparedness. In his book *The Korean War* Hastings reported that more than one-third of South Korea's army vehicles were out of service and indefinitely awaiting repairs because of a lack of spare parts. Hastings wrote that South Korea's vulnerability was compounded by the international political picture: "The withdrawal of American forces from South Korea, the visible lack of enthusiasm within the United States for Syngman Rhee's regime, the opposition of right-wing Republicans to financial aid of any kind for his country, combined with such public statements as that of Acheson to create an overwhelming impression of American indifference to Rhee's fate."

The Truman administration was calling the war "a police action," but a M*A*S*H pilot just back from the front in late 1952 told an audience in Biloxi, Mississippi, "If that's a police action, then it's a tough damn beat and we need a few more cops."

*   *   *   *   *

Like his subordinates in Seoul, President Truman was also enjoying the weekend away from his place of duty. He was back home in Independence, Missouri, when he was notified of the start of hostilities in Korea. He flew back to Washington immediately and ordered American air and sea forces to support the South Korean Army south of the 38th parallel. Three days later, on June 30, he authorized the use of ground forces. The United States was now directly involved in the ground war. Truman also signed Public Law 599, extending the military draft until July 9, 1951, and authorizing the call-up of reserves and National Guard units for up to twenty-one months of service on active duty.

Stalin was just as involved in the war as Truman, even though the Soviet Union itself was officially not in the fighting. "Throughout the initial stage of the Korea War," Dr. Bajanov wrote in 1995, "Stalin was clearly in charge: His word was final on the date of the invasion, he told the Koreans how to fight, and he kept instructing the Sino-Korean command on its every move."

The United Nations called for a cessation of hostilities as soon as the fighting began. When the appeal failed, the U.N. took a historic first step, sending military forces from different nations into the fighting. In all, twenty-two allied nations participated in the Korean War, the first such international force in history. On July 7, MacArthur became the head of the United Nations command, appointed by President Truman.

In another action, fraught with potential as ominous as the developments in Korea, the United States dispatched arms, supplies, and "instructors" to another far-off land unknown to most Americans, one called South Vietnam. Vietnam was another north-south split nation, with a democracy of sorts in the South and a Communist regime across the border in North Vietnam. At the same time, the United States signed a military assistance agreement with France, Cambodia, and Laos, in that part of the world then called "French Indo-China."

*   *   *   *   *

Meanwhile, the men of the SS *Meredith Victory* were preparing to leave Norfolk, Virginia. It was July 28, 1950. The Korean War was now a month old and American troops were fighting along-side the South Korean Army.

Two of the ship's officers were J. Robert Lunney, the staff offi-cer, a product of the Bronx and fresh out of college, and Merl Smith, who had graduated the month before from the United States Merchant Marine Academy at Kings Point on New York's Long Island and was a junior engineer on the ship. We gathered on Sunday afternoon, the evening of Presidents' Day weekend 2000, only four months before the fiftieth anniversary of the start of the war and ten months before the fiftieth anniversary of the Hungnam evacuation, when those two men and their ship made history with extraordinary and repeated acts of heroism and humanitarianism in what has since been called by the United States government "the greatest sea rescue in the history of mankind."

I continued my conversations with Lunney frequently over the next several months. We worked together for a full year as he provided me with background information and descriptions of his own experiences on the *Meredith Victory* and led me to other veterans' organizations, other sources, and other men in different branches of the armed forces who were also at Hungnam. In between my talks with him, I was able to talk to two other officers on the ship—Al Franzon, the ship's third mate, and Al Kaufhold, one of the engineers.

The *Meredith Victory*, named after a small college in North Carolina, was one of the American "victory" ships built during World War II as freighters to help meet the needs of transport-ing supplies and equipment to overseas installations. Hundreds of these ships and their cousins, the "liberty" ships, were built during America's accelerated mobilization program. The victory ships proved especially useful in naval warfare in the Pacific. They were fast and they were small enough to cope with the shallow waters and the severe ebb and flow of the tides of the

Sea of Japan on Korea's east coast and the Yellow Sea on the west.

The *Meredith Victory* had just been reactivated for the new war and her young officers—most of them in their early twenties under their "older" thirty-seven-year-old captain—were eagerly anticipating what they expected to be a cruise of a couple of months. After that, Lunney planned to attend law school at Cornell University. Smith was "going to serve a couple of months and then get a better job" in the maritime service.

As their ship steamed out of the James River and into the Atlantic Ocean, neither man knew their destination. But both guessed that it would have something to do with Korea. They sailed south, across the Gulf of Mexico, then through the Panama Canal, and up the coast of California to Oakland. There they loaded their cargo; their guess about Korea was looking more accurate all the time. They "onloaded" ten Army tanks and 250 trucks, the six-wheelers with a .50-caliber machine gun mounted next to the driver.

All of the equipment was "battle-loaded." The cargo also included 150 tons of ammunition for tanks, small arms, and land mines.

After the crew of the *Meredith Victory* finished loading, the skipper, Captain LaRue, asked Lunney, then twenty-two years old, to come with him. LaRue, who was assuming command of the ship that month after commanding ships in World War II and during the postwar period, told Lunney he had to make three stops in San Francisco before they sailed. They stopped first at the offices of Moore-McCormack Lines, the Merchant Marine company that operated the *Meredith Victory* for its owner, the Maritime Administration, then proceeded to the Military Sea Transportation Service.

Then they made their third stop—Old St. Mary's Church at California and Grant in Chinatown. Captain LaRue wanted to say a prayer for the ship and her men.

As they sailed out of San Francisco and into the Pacific Ocean, the officers and crew of the Meredith Victory left behind a life where their families, friends, and college classmates were singing along with Nat "King" Cole's smash hit, "Mona Lisa," and the other top hits of the day—"A Bushel and a Peck" and a new song with a twist, "Tennessee Waltz," with "That Singing Rage—Miss Patti Page." In the record industry's newest technological advancement, the recording engineers "dubbed" Patti's voice over her own so she was singing harmony with herself. For the men of the *Meredith Victory,* two of the hits of that year held a special irony. Guy Mitchell was bursting onto the scene with a sea chantey, "The Rovin' Kind," and Bing Crosby sang a song with special meaning for them, "May the Good Lord Bless and Keep You."

Television was continuing its inroads into America's everyday life. Color TV was still ten or fifteen years away for most households, but that didn't stop us from heading for the living room—most homes didn't have a "family room"—and watching our ten- or even seven-inch black-and-white screens with delight. There was Sid Caesar and Imogene Coca on *Your Show of Shows,* Jimmy Durante, Jack Benny, and the new shows that season like *Your Hit Parade, I Love Lucy, What's My Line,* and *The Kate Smith Hour.*

If you could afford the price of $189.95, you could buy a brand new Hallicrafter TV set, with its big black-and-white screen of twelve-and-a-half inches, at Phillips store on F Street in Washington. If you didn't have that much spare cash, you could buy it anyhow, for nineteen dollars down and "long, easy credit terms." Still, America's rapidly increasing love for television was not yet reflected in the entertainment section of the daily paper. The radio listings were still longer than those showing the evening's television programs.

However, by 1950, the same year that Walter Cronkite began his career at CBS-TV, television news was becoming a bigger part of our nightly routine. CBS began broadcasting in color for the fortunate few who could afford it. The president of Boston University, Daniel Marsh, saw some danger signals on the horizon in America's obsession with TV that year. "If the television craze continues with the present level of programs," he warned, "we are destined to have a nation of morons." Some farsighted observers of American society saw another change looming in the future. They feared that Americans would begin to get their news from those evening newscasts, which they could watch without having to go to the trouble of actually reading, and abandon that staple of everyday life—the daily newspaper. They were right. Today, with a far larger population, there are 319 fewer daily newspapers published in the United States than there were in 1950.

A young and unknown cartoonist was doing his part to keep Americans entertained by the newspapers. On October 2, 1950, Charles Schulz introduced a syndicated comic strip about cute kids coping with adult problems—the crowd called *Peanuts*, led by Charlie Brown.

The two postwar booms were still flourishing—the baby boom and the housing boom. One builder developed a subdivision in a Maryland suburb of Washington, "beautiful Wheaton Park." A newspaper ad said you could buy a new, three-bedroom home in Wheaton Park with no money down and a mortgage payment of only $58 a month. The ad claimed the homes were "the talk of the town."

If the men sailing out of San Francisco aboard the *Meredith Victory* had a chance to go to the movies in the first half of that year before sailing to the Pacific, they could have seen *Born Yesterday* with Broderick Crawford and Judy Holliday, *Cyrano de Bergerac* starring Jose Ferrer, *The Great Caruso* with the new singing star Mario Lanza, and the story about a harmless dreamer and his imaginary rabbit, *Harvey*, with Jimmy Stewart.

That was the world the men of the *Meredith Victory* left as San Francisco faded into the distance and their ship headed for the unknown.

*   *   *   *   *

The *Meredith Victory*'s orders were to sail to Yokohama, Japan, nonstop. A letter home on August 5 shows that Lunney and his fellow officers had a suspicion about their destination. Several hours before passing through the Panama Canal and maintaining a speed of "close to 17 knots, which is fairly decent speed for these jobs," Lunney speculated:

> It still is not certain as to what we will be carrying or to what port, but in all probability it will be something like tanks or heavy stuff for Japan or Korea. We are under a charter with the Military Sea Transportation Service and our articles read 'to such ports and places in any part of the world as the Master (the captain) may direct or as may be ordered or directed by the United States Government or any department, commission or agency thereof.'

The staff officer then added his own editorial comment: "This pretty well sews up everything from here to the moon!"

Lunney remembers that they arrived in Japan after twelve or thirteen days at sea. There they were ordered to load combat equipment. When they headed out of Tokyo Bay, they opened their sealed orders. Destination: Inchon, on the west coast of South Korea on the Yellow Sea.

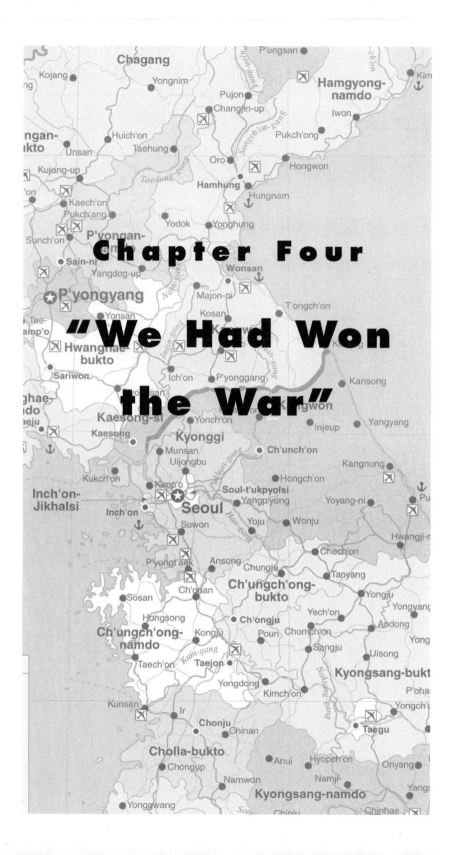

Chapter Four

"We Had Won the War"

With their cargo of "combat-ready" supplies and equipment, the wartime atmosphere aboard ship became even more apparent when the officers and crew learned that they would not be sailing alone. The *Meredith Victory* was part of a convoy of other merchant ships. Obviously a war was in their future, the second in five years for Lunney, a Navy veteran of World War II.

But before the *Meredith Victory* entered battle, a typhoon blew up in the Yellow Sea and the ships of the convoy were forced to disperse. In a letter to home, Bob Lunney described the storm: "The ship just rocked and shook all over . . . We dropped out of the convoy, as had several ships for the same reason the night before."

After the typhoon passed over, Merl Smith says now, "We didn't know where those other freighters were."

Smith also remembers the men's suspicions about what was in store for them. "We didn't know exactly what was up," he said, "but we sensed it was something big. We knew Inchon was enemy territory, so we knew we would be part of an invasion. When we landed at Inchon on September 15, we were one of the first ships to arrive."

The ship lay at anchor until the First Marine Division arrived and secured the beach. Then the *Meredith Victory* was ordered to "offload" her cargo of ammunition and tanks into waiting Navy LSTs.

*   *   *   *   *

It looked as though the war might be over as quickly as MacArthur had boldly predicted, but the winner might be *North Korea*. The invaders rolled through the South and came within thirty miles of pushing the U.N. forces into the sea off the southern tip of the peninsula. But American units, working feverishly, established a defensive perimeter around the port of Pusan, completing their attempts at a stronghold by August 4. Then the first miraculous break occurred—MacArthur's now famous landing at Inchon, where he was able to cut off the North Korean forces, catching them in a pincer movement between his own men at Inchon, halfway up South Korea's west coast, and the U.N. forces still holding the line near Pusan.

Correspondent Bill Lawrence and others—American military officers as well as war correspondents—found that Korea was a different kind of war. As Lawrence wrote in his autobiography, "The war in Korea wasn't the kind of war we had covered in Europe, or I had later covered against the Japanese in the Far Pacific. The war in Korea was a civil war. There were really no distinguishing physical characteristics between friend and foe and it was therefore hard to tell them apart. There was no fixed front line, no rear area that was really safe, and God alone was your guide when you set out to drive a jeep in the general direction of where you thought the main fighting of the moment was in process. . . . In the first three months of the Korean battle, approximately thirty war correspondents were killed, captured, or missing in action."

The *Meredith Victory* reached Inchon on September 15, the day of the invasion. She was the first merchant ship in the convoy to enter the outer harbor. Navy warships were bombarding the beach just ahead of the freighters, which lay at anchor while the men of the First Marine Division secured the beach. The next day the crew of the *Meredith Victory* "offloaded" her combat cargo into waiting LSTs.

"It was an odd coincidence," Lunney wrote in a letter to his family, "that just about the time I should have been starting school, I was in on one of the biggest invasions since Okinawa." His ship put personnel from the Thirty-Second Regimental Combat Team of the Army's Seventh Infantry Division safely ashore on "Blue Beach" at Inchon as part of an invasion force of 230 ships and seventy-thousand men from the United States Army, Navy, and Marines, as well as the Korean Marines.

Two days after the invasion, the *Meredith Victory* found herself caught in an air attack. Two North Korean planes made bombing runs against two warships only five hundred yards away, the USS *Rochester* and a British ship, the HMS *Jamaica*.

"We got lucky," Lunney remembers. "One drop of four bombs became a near-miss off the *Rochester*'s port bow. Three were near misses off her stern, and one bomb hit the *Rochester*, ricocheted off, and caused some damage on deck without exploding. The first plane went on to strafe the *Jamaica*, and wounded three members of her crew before the *Jamaica* shot her down. The second plane escaped."

Merl Smith was on deck when the air attack began. He watched in disbelief as one plane was shot down. "Our guns just disintegrated it," he said.

In a letter back home dated October 9, Lunney told his family about the attack, then added, "I slept through the whole thing."

As the *Meredith Victory* sailed from Inchon after accomplishing her mission, she was approached by a small boat whose occupants, Korean men, were waving a large white flag. They turned out to be North Korean soldiers, thirteen of them, all armed. They were allowed to board the *Meredith Victory*.

Lunney remembers what happened next. "We had some Japanese stevedores on board who spoke Korean," he said, "so they told the soldiers to surrender their arms to us. Then we got the Navy on the radio, and they told us to go to Yokohama, which we did. We were a little nervous about the situation. We were in enemy waters, on an unarmed merchant ship—only they didn't know it. On a merchant ship, the only one with a gun is the captain, and in this case Captain LaRue's weapon was an old .38 revolver. Those soldiers could have captured the ship and all forty-seven of our officers and crew members. Instead, they became what we thought might have been the first POWs caught in the Inchon invasion."

One of the prisoners had been wounded in the head and arms with a knife. Lunney wrote to his family, "I doctored the boy up with sulfa."

The prisoners, it turned out, had been snared in the trap sprung by MacArthur between Inchon and Pusan. "They were ready to surrender to the first American ship they saw," Smith laughed as he recalled. "They just wanted out of the North Korean Army."

To get a better idea of where they came from and to try to find out what they knew, Lunney showed the North Korean soldiers maps of the area. Their reaction convinced the Americans that the soldiers fighting for North Korea were "conscripts," draftees who knew nothing about the war, the reasons for it, where they were, and maybe not even who their enemy was.

"When I showed them those maps," Lunney laughed, "they reacted as if they were looking at the face of the moon."

In the glow of MacArthur's ingenious landing, which was being hailed around the world not only for its success but also for its brilliant strategy, Truman sent a congratulatory telegram to his five-star commander:

> Few operations in military history can match either
> the delaying action where you traded space for time
> in which to build up your forces, or the brilliant
> maneuver which has now resulted in the liberation of
> Seoul . . . Well and nobly done.

The North Koreans were caught in the jaws of a fast-moving vice. American and South Korean troops began a dash back up through South Korea toward Seoul and the 38th parallel, sweeping the enemy out of the way and recapturing everything that had fallen to the North Koreans in the first three months of the war. They reached Seoul within two weeks.

By September 25 MacArthur's brilliant stroke of landing at Inchon had reversed the course of the war and altered its expected outcome to such an extent that the American Joint Chiefs of Staff authorized military operations across the 38th parallel into enemy territory. Truman, Secretary of State Acheson, and Truman's new Secretary of Defense, George C. Marshall, who had taken office only the week before, all concurred in the decision.

Having recaptured all of the South Korean territory that had been lost to the invaders at the start of the war, the United Nations forces, mostly American, embarked on a course to take all of North Korea.

A column by General Carl Spaatz, who retired after serving as a member of the Joint Chiefs of Staff, in *Newsweek* magazine on September 25, from "somewhere in Korea" reflected the euphoria among the American military leaders there. Spaatz predicted, "Unless the North Korean forces receive assistance from Generalissimo Stalin directly and immediately, their days are numbered." Without such help, Spaatz wrote, the North Korean

Army "will be destroyed." He said the landing at Inchon ten days earlier "probably marked the beginning of the end."

Spaatz never mentioned the possibility that the Chinese Communists might enter the war.

In the same issue, a column signed by "The Editors" said an article in the magazine the week before reporting "exclusively" that the United States had submitted proposals to the United Nations General Assembly "in the event of another Korea" was written "in preparation for V-K Day [victory in Korea]."

Amid all the excitement as the U.N. troops swept toward the Yalu River, which marked the northern border between North Korea and Communist China, the Chinese managed to make themselves heard. They voiced a stern warning to the United Nations forces: Do Not Enter. Perhaps emboldened by the first anniversary of the Communist takeover in what was now being called "Red China," its leaders warned that they would take military action if the U.N. troops continued north and became a threat to the Chinese border. But the U.N. troops kept coming. The two fighting forces were on a collision course, one that two months later forced those one hundred thousand refugees to flee their flaming cities, villages, and bombed-out homes in terror and to begin their long, cold, dangerous, and uncertain journey toward the port of Hungnam.

In 1952 one veteran of that fighting said that MacArthur committed a tactical blunder in his race toward the Yalu River in September and October of 1950. "His men were spread a hundred yards apart," he said, "and our supplies couldn't keep up with us. Then the Yalu froze over and those Chinese came charging across into North Korea, blowing bugles and screaming "banzai!"—a Japanese war cry familiar to every man who fought the Japanese in World War II. Oddly enough, it means, 'May you live ten thousand years!'"

General Haig told me, "The debacle of the Chinese entry was less a problem of their entry and more a problem of the strategic surprise they enjoyed. Our forces were all deployed in an extended exploitation demeanor. That was true of the Ninth Corps, which had moved up to the Yalu River, spread all over North Korea, and the same with the X Corps on the right flank. These were isolated units that were totally overwhelmed by masses of Chinese forces. Now, when we got into a configuration where American firepower could be applied in a concentrated way, it was a different picture."

In his 1995 paper, Dr. Bajanov states that by October 1 Stalin was convinced that Red China would have to come to the aid of North Korea because of its rapidly worsening military position. With MacArthur's troops threatening to sweep all of North Korea clear of the enemy, Rhee and his U.N. colleagues would have been able to establish Korea as one united nation.

Dr. Bajanov writes that Stalin sent a message on October 1 to Mao and Chou En-lai, China's prime minister, asking them "to move to the 38th parallel at least 5-6 divisions in order to give our Korean comrades a chance to organize under the protection of your troops." Mao shocked the Kremlin by refusing, claiming that such a move could "drag the Soviet Union into the war with Washington."

Bajanov adds, "The Soviets were stunned with this unexpected change in China's position." However, under continuing pressure from Moscow, China dropped its opposition two weeks later in exchange for a promise from the Soviets that they would provide air power to support the Chinese troops.

President Truman became so concerned about Chinese intervention, with its potential for causing the regional war to erupt into World War III, that he flew across the Pacific to Wake Island in order to meet with MacArthur and put the question to him face-to-face. Truman was literally willing to meet MacArthur more than halfway: the five-star general flew 1,900 miles for the meeting on Wake, while the president of the United States, the general's commander-in-chief, flew 4,700 miles.

Their meeting took place on October 15. In Merle Miller's 1973 oral biography of Truman, *Plain Speaking,* Truman says, "I asked MacArthur point blank if the Chinese would come in, and he said under no circumstances would they come in. He said, 'Mr. President, the war will be over by Thanksgiving, and I'll have the American troops back in Tokyo by Christmas,' and he went on like that." Historian David McCullough said Truman told him that MacArthur said, "We are no longer fearful of their intervention."

Another account verifies the conversations quoted by Miller and McCullough. In Joseph C. Goulden's 1982 book *Korea: The Untold Story of the War,* he quotes from a memo written by Truman on April 4, 1951, a week before he fired MacArthur:

> He again said the Chinese Communists would not attack, that we had won the war and that we could send a division from Korea to Europe in January 1951.

In defense of MacArthur it should be pointed out that America's new Central Intelligence Agency (the CIA) also did not expect the Chinese to enter the war. The CIA conducted a special analysis and concluded that intervention by China was not "probable," barring a major development such as a decision by Stalin to start World War III.

It was a disastrous miscalculation. The Korean War lasted almost another three years.

MacArthur was a victim of more than his own misjudgment. Like any commander or any other executive, his judgment and decisions were only as good as the information that he received. There is evidence today that not only were the Chinese ready to enter the war, they already had.

Although different sources offer different dates, testimony from Chinese prisoners of war later revealed that Chinese troops entered North Korea at least the day before the Truman-MacArthur meeting and maybe even earlier. Several accounts say that 120,000 Chinese Communist troops from the Fourth Field Army had already crossed the Yalu, with many of them manning Russian artillery and driving Russian-made tanks. But MacArthur and his staff apparently were unaware of the Chinese movements into North Korea.

MacArthur and his intelligence chief, Major General Charles Willoughby, needed only to listen to their own officers to learn what the Chinese might be expected to do. Colonel J. F. McAllister, an Air Force pilot who flew reconnaissance missions into China, talked to *U.S. News & World Report* magazine for a special report in its June 25, 1990 issue, in a cover story headed:

40 YEARS AFTER KOREA—
THE FORGOTTEN WAR

"We had forecast that the Chinese were coming in," Colonel McAllister said. "When we flew up across the Yalu, we told them [in Tokyo] there was a hell of a bunch of Chinese on the other side."

U.S. News went so far in its special report as to charge that MacArthur and his senior officers knew the Chinese were entering the war but tried to suppress the evidence. The magazine article quoted Robert Martin, a former foreign editor for the magazine who covered the war for CBS, as saying he remembered one captured soldier "who had a very, very broad Sichuan accent, so he clearly wasn't some North Chinese who had just come across the border to help. Willoughby kept saying they were Koreans born in Manchuria. I told him, 'Look, I talked to these guys in Chinese.' He just looked away. I really think he knew but didn't want to know."

In the 1990 article *U.S. News* claimed, "MacArthur could barely disguise his desire for a confrontation with China that would force President Truman to let him carry the war into Manchuria. Four decades later the evidence suggests that, for his own purposes, he deliberately suppressed intelligence that might have averted the disaster at Chosin and prevented thousands of American casualties."

The magazine could have added that if the course of the war in the North had been different and the crisis at the Chosin Reservoir had been averted, the evacuation of Hungnam might never have been necessary. Thousands of lives on both sides would have been saved and almost one hundred thousand refugees—the pitiful old men, women of every age with their children and grandchildren on their backs and in their arms and at their breasts, and the kids themselves—might never have become refugees at all.

The magazine article claimed that an unidentified "key Truman administration foreign policy aide" told their reporter that, "The problem was not that we lacked good intelligence, but that we were getting dishonest interpretations of good intelligence by a crazy man who wanted to get us into a full-scale war with the Chinese."

General Haig offers a different explanation. He told me the United States "misjudged China because of our failure to communicate with its leaders from the beginning. I sat in on the telecom between MacArthur and Harry Truman. Both MacArthur and Truman, for reasons which bothered me as a young first lieutenant, suddenly drew a line around the Pescadore Islands, and MacArthur then ordered a team to Taiwan to open up the military assistance program. When you combine that with crossing the 38th parallel [the advance by the United Nations forces after their landing at Inchon], you see why the Chinese concluded—because we didn't let them know what we were doing—that we were going to reinstall Chiang Kai-shek on the mainland and overthrow the revolution. That's why they entered that war. Hell, it was the Russians who were running that war."

During our interview, General Haig said he thought that both President Truman and General MacArthur made that mistake.

China's entry into the war changed not only the war itself but also the attitude of the American people toward it. Harry G. Summers Jr., in his *Korean War Almanac,* reports that 75 percent of those Americans surveyed at the start of the war agreed with President Truman's decision to send in troops. However, after the Chinese entered the war, support dropped in November to 50 percent and stayed there for the rest of the three-year war.

Summers also writes that 65 percent of those surveyed in June said the war was not a mistake, but that after the Chinese entered, the reverse was true—65 percent said it *was* a mistake. By the time Dwight Eisenhower ran for president in 1952 to succeed Truman, only one-third of Americans thought the war was worth fighting. By the time of the truce in July 1953, that figure had dropped to 25 percent.

In his 1990 Almanac, Summers wrote, "American public opinion during the Korean War followed almost exactly the same pattern it would follow in the Vietnam War, except that the loss of public support was far quicker in the Korean War than it was in the Vietnam War." Truman's term expired only eighteen months after the war started, and he declined to seek reelection.

Summers wrote that at that time, Truman's disapproval ratings "were much higher than President Lyndon Johnson's ever were," even though Johnson served as president for five years during the Vietnam War.

Chapter Five

A National Emergency in America

After the Chinese entered the war, MacArthur launched an all-out offensive on November 24. "If successful," he said in another of his bold predictions, "this should for all practical purposes end the war, restore peace and unity to Korea . . . and enable the prompt withdrawal of United Nations forces."

On November 28, more than two hundred thousand additional Chinese troops charged across the Yalu in a massive counteroffensive. U.N. forces, mostly Americans, retreated in confusion in what some have suggested was the worst military reversal in U.S. history up to that time. At 6:15 A.M. Omar Bradley called Truman at the Blair House, the residence across Pennsylvania Avenue from the White House. Truman was staying there while the executive mansion underwent urgently needed repairs. Only four weeks earlier, on November 1, he had survived an assassination attack when two Puerto Rican nationalists stormed Blair House and killed a Secret Service guard before they were thwarted. One of the terrorists was also killed. Bradley told Truman he had "a terrible message" from MacArthur. At a hastily called staff meeting later that morning, Truman said, "We've got a terrible situation on our hands. The Chinese have come in with both feet." He said it was the worst news he'd had since becoming president five and a half years before.

To meet this massive and unexpected threat, MacArthur wanted reinforcements on a major scale as well as a naval blockade of

China and bombing of the Chinese mainland. Instead of expanding the war into a much larger one, the National Security Council, in a 3:00 P.M. meeting that same day, voted to "contain" the war to Korea and avoid the risk of giving Stalin and company justification for spreading the hostilities to other parts of Asia and, worse yet, into a third world war.

The fate of the U.N. forces changed almost overnight. MacArthur ordered a "withdrawal" from the North, back toward South Korea. The up-and-back-and-up again war was headed back again—south, over territory the American-led U.N. troops had just captured after Inchon. The withdrawal reflected the deterioration of the overall situation. With Christmas approaching, Americans back home were reading headlines that grew more alarming each day. *The Washington Post* ran a newspaper rarity, an eight-column, three-line banner line, on December 1 that read:

TRUMAN PONDERS A-BOMB, HASN'T ORDERED IT; ATLEE COMING HERE; REDS VETO KOREA ULTIMATUM; GIs AND MARINES CAUGHT IN NEW CHINESE TRAPS

On the same day, Stalin sent a cable to Mao that read in part:

> Your success makes happy not only myself and my comrades in the leadership, but the entire Soviet people. Let me welcome from all my heart you and your friends in the leadership, your army and the entire Chinese people in connection with tremendous successes in the struggle against American troops.

The success that was causing Stalin to rejoice continued and the situation facing MacArthur's troops grew still more desperate at an alarming rate. On November 30, Alexander Haig's boss, General Almond, the commander of the Army's

X Corps, ordered his troops to withdraw to the Hungnam perimeter. On December 9, MacArthur ordered the United Nations forces to evacuate by sea from Hungnam. The Navy and Marines were ready to carry out the order. They had been preparing for an evacuation by sea from Hungnam for a week.

Rumors spread quickly among the North Korean civilians that the Americans were also willing to evacuate as many of them as possible. Refugees began fleeing on foot toward Hungnam from miles away. Others quickly caught trains. When the last train pulled out of Hamhung for Hungnam, fifty thousand refugees— more than half of the city's population—fought to climb on board. Many of those traveling by foot from more remote areas and carrying their children were killed along the twenty miles from Koto-Ri to Hungnam when they walked through mine fields and even the front lines despite repeated warnings from the United Nations forces about the dangers they would encounter.

The shocking number of refugees complicated the military withdrawal. They clogged the roads to Hungnam. They were a pitiful sight. A thick government report, *Third Infantry Division in Korea,* described their pathetic appearance along the roadside: "Even their grief, destitution and poverty also became commonplace because they were seen everywhere. The country was stricken with war. Its people were weary with its misery and fear."

*   *   *   *   *

One of the refugees traveling south on foot along the roads of North Korea, the Reverend Sun Myung Moon, later founded the Unification Church and became publisher of *The Washington*

Times. He had been imprisoned by the North Korean government for preaching religion in that Communist country, which did not tolerate religious beliefs and practices to the extent that they are accepted in democratic societies.

Reverend Moon, like most Koreans from both the North and the South, was conditioned to survive extreme hardships. His parents were farmers with eight children. In September 1947, when Reverend Moon was in his twenties, the North Korean police arrested him for preaching religion on the streets of Pyongyang. In April 1948 he was put on trial for "advocating chaos in society." Handcuffed and with his head shaved, he was convicted in a trial that lasted one day. He was imprisoned and sentenced to five years at Tong Nee, a concentration camp in Hungnam for political prisoners. As prisoner number 586, he recognized his prison term as a death sentence—the life expectancy for prisoners in that camp ranged from six months to three years.

Conditions in the camp were inhuman. Prisoners were rationed only one cup of rice and one cup of water a day. Reverend Moon gave half of each to his fellow prisoners. Prisoners occasionally died while gagging on their food. Other prisoners were so desperate that they would reach down the throat of the dead prisoner to retrieve any unswallowed rice and eat it themselves. Most of those who died had simply given up. The future pastor was determined that if he was going to die, he would do so only on his own terms, not those of his captors.

Moon remained in the concentration camp for two and a half years and survived an attack of malaria. With the stoicism that is the trademark of the Korean people—and prayers—Reverend Moon endured. "I never prayed from weakness," he said later. "I never complained. I was never angry at my situation. I never even asked His help, but was always busy comforting Him and telling Him not to worry about me."

As the United Nations forces came closer to Hungnam for the first time in mid-October, the guards began executing prisoners. When the U.N. troops got even closer, the guards panicked and ran out of the camp to save their own lives—without worrying that the prisoners would be able to escape, too.

On October 14 Reverend Moon walked to freedom and kept on walking. Instead of hoping for a ship to carry him south from Hungnam—there were none in the harbor at that time—he walked out of the city and headed for Pyongyang, one hundred miles away. In early December he left Pyongyang for Seoul, still on foot and this time accompanied by two followers, Jung Hua Pak and Won Pil Kim.

They walked on primitive roads and through mountain passes, their trip made even harder because of the ice and snow, the soldiers with their combat equipment and military vehicles, and all the desperate refugees trying to escape from the Chinese and North Korean Armies. All three remained aware that if caught they would be beheaded. Pak broke his leg. Reverend Moon carried him on his back. With no food and in subzero temperatures, they covered eighteen miles a day. At one point they had to cross part of the Yellow Sea to an island, with Pak still on Reverend Moon's back.

They arrived in Seoul on Christmas Eve. Reverend Moon had traveled five hundred miles on foot in a journey to freedom and safety.

Reverend Moon, now eighty years old, still feels gratitude toward the American troops who saved his life, even this many years later. On February 2, 2000, he delivered the commemorative address for the presentation of the American Century Awards. The awards are presented by *The Washington Times* Foundation, which he founded to recognize individuals who are, in his words, "champions who through your service have made significant contributions to improving the quality of life for all Americans."

Speaking at the Cannon House office building in Washington before members of the Senate and the House of Representatives and the diplomatic corps, Moon said, "I am grateful that God gave me the opportunity to serve America, because American-led U.N. forces, in the process of saving my country during the Korean War, liberated me from a Communist concentration camp where I had been imprisoned for preaching the word of God."

*　　*　　*　　*　　*

The withdrawing American soldiers and Marines were forced to reevaluate their attitudes toward the North Korean civilians in the midst of the mass exodus toward Hungnam. "The baggy clothes and long outer garments of Korean civilians, once considered only with curiosity, came to be observed with suspicion," the report on the Third Division said. "At check points and guard posts, Koreans were examined carefully by MPs and Korean police. The voluminous clothes were found many times to conceal weapons or to cover the uniform of a soldier of the NKPA [North Korean People's Army]. Enemy agents were picked up, often including women and even children, who were required to count U.N. soldiers and weapons and return with their information to their superiors. American soldiers came to grow fidgety when civilians were in the vicinity, particularly when they were in the rear or to the flanks. A farmer and his wife working about a farmhouse deserved watching; the stack of wood with which they labored might be just the winter fuel supply, or it might be the hiding place for weapons and ammunition. Patrols became adept at probing in culverts, rice stacks and other likely spots for hidden caches of arms."

The actual evacuation began on December 10, when the First Marine Division arrived in Hungnam. The Marines were not alone. The refugees who complicated their withdrawal along the way also streamed into the city from the surrounding towns, villages, and countryside. Jung Park, the seventeen-year-old schoolgirl, and her mother were among them. Jung admits today that they were among the "lucky" ones because they did not have to walk miles to Hungnam. They traveled some forty miles but were able to ride in a truck brought to them by one of her brothers, a member of the South Korean Army, whose unit was in the area.

Jung Park and her mother slipped out of their hiding place in North Korea under the cover of darkness at midnight on a night in the first half of December. They had been hiding from their own army after their home on their small rice farm had been bombed out. Several families hid together in a neighbor's house until they began the trip to Hungnam. The harsh North Korean winter added to their burden. "It was raining and snowing, and the wind was blowing," Jung Park said in her flower shop in Maryland. "North Korea weather in the winter is like Chicago."

She carried her school bag with only a few earthly possessions as well as her brother's guitar and accordion. The fighting on the beach would not start for several more days, so there was a silence. "We were afraid to make any noise," she said. As some of the first refugees to reach the dock at Hungnam, the schoolgirl and her mother, who was in her midfifties, had to grab the first available means of transportation—a small fishing boat. That's when they had to throw everything overboard. "That ship was almost sinking," she said. "They told us they could take only humans, no possessions."

Eventually the fishing boat bobbed and weaved its way to Mukho, another port approximately halfway down the coast of the Sea of Japan between Hungnam and Pusan, where the refugees waited for a much larger, safer, and more comfortable means of transportation, a Navy LST. One became available several days later. LSTs are not normally considered an upgrade in sailing accommodations, but to the refugees in that fishing boat, it must have seemed like the *Queen Mary*.

Jung and her mother ate their Christmas meal aboard the LST. "It was the first time I ever had spaghetti," she said. "And tomato sauce."

Was it good?

"Yes. Very. I was hungry."

*   *   *   *   *

The other schoolgirl, Soon Park, arrived at Hungnam with her classmates and was guided onto a waiting LST. The ship did not leave Hungnam for several days and Soon and her friends from Hamhung could do nothing but patiently wait in one of the lower holds of the ship. "We were at least warm," she said when I talked to her in March 2000, "but others were on the deck, and they were so cold." Soon and her classmates climbed their way back up to the deck and witnessed the "bombardment" along the beach during the evacuation. "It was like fireworks," she says today. The young schoolgirl witnessed another grim sight of war when the LST pulled into Mukho, where the bodies of several refugees were dumped overboard after they died from the paralyzing combination of extreme cold and hunger. "I saw that," Soon said.

After reaching safety in the south, Soon asked everyone she met about the fate of her family back in North Korea. Eventually she encountered one refugee who said she had been on the last train out of Hamhung bound for Hungnam, as those fifty thousand North Korean men, women, and children were clamoring to climb on board. The woman told Soon that her parents had not been on the train. Forty years later, Soon found out that her whole family had stayed behind. By that time they were all deceased, even her only brother, who was younger than Soon.

*   *   *   *   *

Who were these North Koreans, the civilians of the enemy, for whom American men were fighting and dying?

Stanley Bolin's follow-up report twenty-five years later said, "They and their families had belonged to a group not welcomed by the leftist revolutionary movement in the North. They were anti-Communist political activists, land owners, businessmen and educators. A few of them had served as public officials after the United Nations forces had pushed the Communist Armies out of the North and into Manchuria. As members of the newly established local government and of the Youth Corps, they had helped to restore peace and public order under the U.N. Command. Their dream of national unification seemed to have been realized at last."

The intervention by the Chinese changed all that, just as it changed the rest of the war. By the time the Chinese had forced U.N. troops into a pocket around Hungnam, "several hundred thousand refugees" were trapped, according to Bolin's report. Most of them had fled from their homes because they feared the Chinese soldiers. Suddenly they were trapped and under siege in the beleaguered port area while the defense perimeter around it, manned by the U.S. Seventh and Third Infantry Divisions, was shrinking at an alarming pace.

Bolin described the scene at Hungnam in graphic terms: "It was the 10th of December 1950. Just offshore from the port of Hungnam, and stretching in a line out to sea, were . . . vessels of all types. They formed a fleet of 193 ships and were about to take part in the largest military evacuation in history."

At the same time, the U.S. Army was producing heroes of its own. One came in for special mention by Stan Swinton, a reporter for the Associated Press, who wrote from Korea, "A stubby, two-star general named Robert H. Soule is the man of the hour here. Soule is the human dynamo who commands the Third Infantry Division. And the Johnny-come-lately Third has emerged as the fighting heart of this besieged beachhead." Swinton reported that General Soule performed under his own personal slogan, which he recommended to everyone under his command: "Get tough." Swinton also said in his dispatch that Soule's favorite advice to his troops was, "Shoot back. As long as you're firing at them, they're not going to shoot at you."

*   *   *   *   *

As British Prime Minister Clement Atlee prepared to fly to Washington and Americans flocked downtown to department stores to do their Christmas shopping in those last years before suburban shopping malls, *The Washington Post*'s Marshall Andrews reported on December 15 that Truman would declare a state of national emergency the next day. Andrews also predicted that Truman, in a presidential address to the nation that night, "will tell his countrymen the hour of the crisis is here, and they must now get down to the work for which they have been rolling up their sleeves."

Andrews was right. Truman declared a state of national emergency the next day, calling for a large increase in military strength, economic stabilization to put production on a wartime footing, and the establishment of controls on wages and prices. The Selective Service was drafting eighty thousand men a month into the armed forces, leading to a total of 5.7 million American men and women in uniform around the world during the Korean War.

Truman issued an executive order on December 16 establishing an Office of Defense Mobilization headed by Charles E. Wilson, who earned $175,000 a year as president of General Electric. His new salary for helping to repel this grave Communist threat was $22,500. Truman's executive order gave Wilson "a grant of powers almost without precedent in American history," according to one source. The executive order directed Wilson to "direct, control and coordinate all mobilization activities of the executive branch of the government, including but not limited to production, procurement, manpower and transport activities."

Secretary of Defense George C. Marshall, the former Army chief of staff, later said, "We were at our lowest point." Some people were already calling the hostilities in Korea "World War Two and a Half."

The headlines in the world's papers continued to tell the story. As a wartime environment gripped the nation and the world, *The Washington Post* displayed another three-line, eight-column banner line:

NATION THREATENED, TRUMAN SAYS; CONTROLS NEAR; HOUSE PASSES $17 BILLION TO SPEED DEFENSES; REDS SMASHING AT BEACHHEAD IN NORTHEAST KOREA

In the withdrawal, the Chinese trapped many of the one hundred thousand American soldiers and Marines 135 miles above the 38th parallel, near the Chosin Reservoir. The nation followed their fate anxiously, with many of us watching on our new television sets as two of the first network news anchors, Douglas Edwards on CBS and John Cameron Swayze on NBC, brought word of their fate, illustrated by grainy, black-and-white still photographs, primitive maps, and newsreels of the fighting and the "withdrawal."

Our troops were making their way along a winding, mountainous route toward Hamhung, the political, commercial, and educational center of the province, and the port at Hungnam. They carried what supplies and equipment they could, plus their weapons, in temperatures that plunged to forty degrees below zero at night in the mountains, in snow drifts sometimes ten feet deep, with howling winds blasting them in the face over twelve tortuous days—all while under enemy fire.

*   *   *   *   *

The Chinese People's Liberation Army Academy of Military Science in Beijing published an "after-action report" on this period of the fighting in 1988. One excerpt graphically describes the fury of the fighting and the severity of the weather. It reads in part, "The enemy [meaning U.S. forces] fled to Koto-ri [between the reservoir and Hungnam] on December 7. At 0700 hours [7:00 A.M.] on the 8th, they continued to break out southward, supported by a large amount of air force [the U.S. Air Force], and were blocked by two companies of our 58th Division on a narrow road south of Koto-ri. At this time, the enemy on the one hand fiercely attacked to seize the road, in coordination with a large amount of air force, and on the other hand, sent enemy . . . northward to reinforce and come to their aid. Our defending troops in a bitter cold of around 30 degrees below zero fought stubbornly. Heavy fighting went on all day."

The report continued, "We [the Chinese] destroyed over 800 enemy and blocked reinforcement coming to the aid . . . The enemy broke through our positions on the 9th and continued to flee south. Our 20th Army's 89th Division cut off and destroyed over 600 enemy and attacked and destroyed or captured more than 90 motor vehicles . . . On the 12th, the U.S. 3rd Division came north from Oro-ri to reinforce and come to their aid. The fleeing enemy broke out of our army's encirclement and fled to Oro-ri."

The subzero temperatures compounded by the strong winds prompted some of the GIs to joke that the biting, bone-chilling North Korean winter weather was "straight from Siberia, just like everything else the Commies are using."

*　　*　　*　　*　　*

Colonel Fred Long, then a young officer in the Third Infantry Division, said in a 1997 article for the Seventh Infantry Regiment Association, "The harsh and continuous cold was an implacable enemy. It froze rifle bolts and split gun barrels. It sapped batteries, congealed oil so that engines wouldn't start, froze the ground and broke mortar base plates, made digging foxholes virtually impossible. It was cold which drained men's strength and numbed their minds. And it was cold comfort indeed to know that the enemy suffered as much or more from the unremitting, hellish cold."

On Christmas Eve, under the command of Colonel John Guthrie, Long's Seventh Regiment came across Pink Beach at Hungnam and boarded landing craft that took them out in the harbor to a Navy troop transport waiting to take them out of danger.

"Several Marines and sailors in the Beachmaster's Party were killed along with a few of the 7th's troops crossing the beach,"

Long wrote. "Under Guthrie's calm leadership, the temporary chaos was controlled and the beach was cleared without further incident. Colonel Guthrie and those of us in his Command Party were in the last landing craft to leave the beach. These were the last American soldiers to leave Hungnam and North Korea."

Chapter Six
"A Striking Sight"

As the withdrawal of the U.S. units continued, so did the unbroken and unending human chain of North Korea's old men, women of all ages, and children. They were falling in with the U.N. forces and withdrawing with them, willing to leave their homeland behind for the possibility of a safer and happier life elsewhere, even though they had no idea of where the withdrawal might take them. Lieutenant Colonel Roy E. Appleman described the experience in his 1990 book *Escaping the Trap: The U.S. Army X Corps in Northeast Korea, 1950,* calling it a "striking" sight as one hundred thousand refugees fell in with the U.N. forces. Their presence was a threat to their own safety as well as the safety of the troops. "It constituted an immediate serious military threat," Appleman wrote, "because enemy troops habitually infiltrated these civilian groups, either as spies and saboteurs or to launch sudden disruptive attacks whenever the opportunity arose." He said the problem became "severe" as the withdrawing columns of American troops slowly wound their way through the snow-covered mountains toward the sea.

It was the longest and largest withdrawal in American military history.

Americans back home breathed easier in the knowledge that their sons and brothers and husbands and boyfriends had survived, at least most of them. The toll was high, with 4,395 casualties. The First Marine Division alone suffered over 2,000 casualties—342 dead, 78 missing in action, and 1,683 wounded. Their dead were buried in several ceremonies, one at a Marine cemetery near Hungnam on December 13, with Major General O. P. Smith, their commander, rendering the final salute.

General Haig doesn't remember the event as a "withdrawal." In his autobiography he wrote, "However orderly this withdrawal, it was a retreat, and the men felt it. So would the unfortunate civilians we left behind."

During the evacuation, Haig flew over the chaotic scene at Hungnam in a light liaison plane, an L-19, while General Almond did the same in another L-19. They each witnessed the scene since described by those on the ground or on ships in the harbor. Haig later wrote, "Masses of refugees carrying their meager belongings had intermingled with our troops during the withdrawal. It was clear to every soldier and marine that these people were desperate to escape the returning Communist regime. Just how desperate became unforgettably apparent near the end when, on looking down from our small planes while flying over the harbor at Hungnam, we saw tens of thousands of civilians wading through the freezing surf toward American ships lying at anchor in the harbor."

General Almond and his young aide-de-camp talked back and forth over the radio from their light planes as they circled the harbor. While they watched the overpowering human struggle below, General Almond said to Haig, who had been promoted to captain in October, "We can't leave those people. Take care of that, Haig."

Fifty years later I kidded General Haig about that order from Almond, saying that he knows from his own experience, both as a lieutenant and as a four-star general, that generals can do that—look at a complicated, seemingly hopeless situation and say to their junior officer simply, "Take care of that." And the officer will.

Haig did, and he never considered the order an act of cowardice or ducking responsibility on Almond's part. The commander was simply doing what good senior executives, in the military and in civilian life, do—delegate authority. "He was good at that," Haig laughed as we talked, "and it wasn't because he didn't have any guts. I had to tackle him several times to get him out of the line of fire."

He laughed more as he described another incident in the thick of the war when he had to get Almond out of the line of fire, literally. "That's what happened when we rode the back of a tank into a Chinese machine gun nest and they started pinging rounds off of us," he said. "After the U.N. withdrawal to the south, we headed back north and were on a tank when we started getting shot at. We were on the back, so I all but dragged him off the back of the tank and told him to stay behind me while I climbed back up on the tank and directed its guns to knock out the machine gun nest."

Almond was never afraid of combat, Haig said. "This guy spent every day where the action was heaviest with a combat unit. I probably saw more fire as an aide than I ever would as a platoon leader," he chuckled, "because wherever the action was, that's where he was. That meant that at night, when I'd come back, usually dead tired, I'd write his diary. Then I would go to the staff and get things done that had to be done."

Marine Colonel Edward Forney, one of the Corp's leading amphibious experts, was directing the operations on the beach at Hungnam from his headquarters in a shed near the dock. Forney was General Almond's deputy chief of staff and was in charge of the evacuation itself, including loading the troops onto the ships, evacuating the refugees from the beach safely onto anything that would float, and removing or destroying any supplies or equipment that could be of value to the onrushing enemy forces. He worked closely with Colonel Rowny, the corps logistician.

Haig communicated with Forney and Rowny and made certain that those responsible for getting enough ships up to Hungnam to carry out the evacuation would do so. Even though Haig was a young junior officer, he was already wise in the ways of getting things done in the military. When requesting the necessary number of ships from senior officers he made sure that "they were aware of the General's strong view about that." Haig said he "passed the word, and somehow Colonel Forney found the ships to transport some one hundred thousand of them [the refugees] to freedom."

The evacuation of so many civilian refugees did not happen automatically or without dramatic debate. It happened only after behind-the-scenes, back-and-forth deliberations among U.S. officials who had to consider whether to risk American lives for such an unprecedented operation. Dr. Bong Hak Hyun described the debate in *Christmas Cargo: A Civilian Account of the Hungnam Evacuation*, written with Marian Hyun. Dr. Hyun, a civil affairs adviser to General Almond, later became a professor of pathology and hematology at Thomas Jefferson University Hospital in Philadelphia.

Dr. Hyun convinced Colonel Forney to talk to General Almond and plead for evacuating the North Korean refugees from Hungnam instead of abandoning them. When Forney finally agreed to talk to Almond, he told Hyun, "Doc, it's going to be difficult, but let's give it a try." When he saw a worried look on Hyun's face, Forney added, "Napoleon didn't find the word 'impossible' in his dictionary."

On November 30 Forney and Hyun met with Almond. Hyun pressed the issue, knowing there was still strong opposition to taking the extra time to evacuate the North Koreans and risk the loss of American lives. He told Almond, "You have people here who really believe in democracy, sir. They've fought against the Communists for the past five years. You must help them, sir."

Colonel Forney added, "Sir, they have risked their lives by cooperating with us."

Hyun continued, "And what about the people who've been working for the U.N. troops?" He said they should not be abandoned for reasons of military expediency.

Almond heard them out, then said "Agreed. But at this point, I'm not even sure our *own* troops can be evacuated." Almond also expressed his concern about the possibility that the enemy might infiltrate the thousands of refugees with spies, a fear shared by many in command positions.

When the give-and-take was over, Almond agreed only that he would talk to General Headquarters in Tokyo.

Dr. Hyun continued to plead his case. He met with General Almond several more times, pestering him about the civilian evacuation. Colonel Forney and Major James Short, chief of the historical section, continued to support Hyun.

Hyun's case appeared lost on December 9 when the Army announced it would not be able to evacuate Korean civilian employees. "I was beginning to feel as helpless as those who were coming to see me," Dr. Hyun said, "and almost as desperate."

However, Dr. Hyun met four days later with a priest, Father Patrick Cleary, a Maryknoll missionary to Korea who had been assigned to the X Corps as a Catholic chaplain. Through a South Korean contact, Father Cleary and Dr. Hyun came up with two LSTs to evacuate equipment from Hungnam so other ships would be available to carry out four thousand refugees. It was mid-December. The deadline for the evacuation of Hamhung, only eight miles away, had been set for six o'clock the next morning. The Chinese troops were now just outside the city.

On the afternoon of December 15 General Almond told a meeting attended by Colonel Forney and Dr. Hyun, "We'll evacuate four thousand to five thousand civilians from Hamhung to Hungnam by train."

When Dr. Hyun stopped at a Presbyterian church to spread the word he found fifty parishioners praying in the basement, thinking this would be their last night of prayer together. The Chinese were expected by morning. When he told them the Americans would evacuate them to safety, one of them hollered, "Moses has come to evacuate us!" The rest of the worshippers picked up the cry and began repeating it in a chant.

Dr. Hyun visited the home of a friend he had known since elementary school and urged him to take his wife and hurry to the train station so they could be evacuated. But the man's wife was about to deliver a baby and refused to leave. Later Dr. Hyun was almost overcome with sadness at having to abandon his friend and his friend's wife. "I kept thinking that somehow I should have forced him and his wife to go," he said, "and I cried for having failed him." Some of the leading anti-Communists in North Korea were evacuated, along with most of the Christian population, but many others were left behind at Hamhung, according to Dr. Hyun.

"The train, which finally pulled out at 2:00 A.M., arrived in Hungnam at 5:00 A.M.," he said. "Many of those who had been unable to board the train tried to walk through frozen rice fields and mountain roads to Hungnam. Of these, more than half were stopped and forced to turn back by the MPs to keep the roads clear for military vehicles and prevent spies from leaving the area. Despite the MPs, many civilians did reach Hungnam, including refugees from all over the northeast."

With the evacuation of Hamhung complete, the next challenge was what to do with the one hundred thousand refugees who had traveled into Hungnam and waited for days to board ships. The lucky ones were housed in abandoned schools or individual homes with no heat. The less fortunate simply had to wait outdoors in schoolyards and other places of assembly, with no heat, water, or cooking facilities. Some died. Others gave birth.

Meanwhile the ships were arriving to evacuate the military personnel. In a port intended to accommodate only seven ships at one time, eleven of them rode at anchor. "The military evacuation went on day and night," Dr. Hyun recalled, "with sailors continuously repairing damaged port facilities and broken-down tugboats. The temperature dropped to -10°C [14 degrees Fahrenheit]. The sound of gunfire was getting closer, and still no boats were in sight for the civilians."

Relief finally arrived on December 17 or 18, when three LSTs from the South Korean Navy arrived at Hungnam, followed by a half dozen transports from Japan. The civilian evacuation began on December 19. The LSTs carried far greater numbers than their official capacity, more than five thousand passengers on ships built to carry one thousand. One ship reportedly carried out ten thousand North Koreans.

Dr. Hyun was ordered aboard the *Sergeant Andrew Miller* on December 21. He watched all night on deck as the evacuation continued. Some refugees panicked, terrified that there might not be enough room for them. Their fears were compounded by the booming sounds of war as the enemy closed in. At night, Dr. Hyun said the naval gunfire was "like shooting stars falling on the horizon."

Dr. Hyun's ship pulled out of Hungnam harbor on the morning of December 22, the day before the *Meredith Victory* sailed. "That evening," he remembered, "I could still see and hear gunfire, even though we were far from Hungnam."

When Colonel Forney told him later that one hundred thousand refugees had been rescued off the beach of Hungnam, Dr. Hyun was overcome with emotion. "I tried to thank him, but was unable to speak," he said. "The X Corps had helped more people than I would ever have thought possible." Colonel Forney was transferred back to the States soon after the evacuation and Dr. Hyun wrote him a letter of gratitude. Colonel Forney wrote back, "I will never forget the look on your face when you knew that over 100,000 from your own part of the country had been saved. That look was sufficient thanks."

The rescue could not have happened much later. The nearby city of Wonsan was in enemy hands, blocking off any possible evacuation to the south, and no airplanes were available for civilians. The sea was the only way out of Hungnam. Several ships were waiting for them.

One of those ships was the SS *Meredith Victory*.

She had been making shuttle runs to Inchon, Pusan, and Japan through the fall and was ordered to deliver ten thousand tons of jet fuel in fifty-two-gallon drums from Tokyo to the Marine Air Wing at Yonpo Airfield near Hungnam. By the time they arrived at Hungnam, a major port on the Sea of Japan, the men of the *Meredith Victory* found they were unable to unload the fuel because of heavy enemy pressure. The Marines were evacuating.

The ship was ordered to Pusan to discharge the fuel. While there, but before they could finish offloading the fuel, Captain LaRue received emergency orders to return to Hungnam immediately to aid in the evacuation. The *Meredith Victory* arrived at Hungnam on the evening of December 20.

American troops were still waiting to be evacuated from Hungnam, so every available ship was needed there. In addition, there were those North Korean refugees, almost one hundred thousand of them. They were the women, children, and old men of the enemy, but they were human beings nevertheless. What was to become of them?

When the *Meredith Victory* steamed into the outer harbor at Hungnam, she was met by a Navy minesweeper that was to escort the freighter to a point closer to the beach, where the refugees were clamoring for a trip to safety. Staff Officer Lunney remembers that the minesweeper flashed a signal asking what kind of cargo was on board. That form of communication, with a crewmember blinking signals through a set of slats over a spotlight, was necessary because all American ships were under radio silence. Russian submarines were lurking below the water's surface.

"When we signaled to them that we were carrying jet fuel," Lunney said, "we could almost see the shock on their faces."

The sweeper was essential because the *Meredith Victory* was steaming into what today is still considered one of the heaviest minefields in the history of naval warfare. "They had laid down every kind of mine imaginable," Lunney said. "Magnetic mines, lured mines, 'counter mines,' which count the number of ships passing overhead and then explode after every fifth or tenth ship or whatever they're set for. Today we would call them 'smart mines.' They also had 'pressure mines,' which respond to the size of the ship passing the mine. And a lot of the mines were the old World War II horned mines, the kind you see in the movies."

Under orders to maintain a distance of 2,500 yards between herself and the minesweeper, the officers of the *Meredith*

Victory quickly noticed that the distance between the two ships was increasing. "The sweeper kept pulling away," Lunney said. "They didn't want anything to do with our jet fuel."

As the freighter lay at anchor off the beach, several U.S. Army colonels came on board. One of them, Colonel John H. Chiles of the Army's X Corps, served under General Almond. The colonels met with Captain LaRue and some of his officers, including Staff Officer Lunney, in the "saloon," the gathering place on a ship called the "ward room" in Navy lingo. Colonel Chiles asked Captain LaRue if he would be willing to take some of the refugees off the beach and carry them back to Pusan since his ship was one of the last in the harbor.

Lunney's memory of LaRue's response remains undimmed by the years. "They described the situation and told Captain LaRue that the evacuation of Hungnam had already begun, which we didn't know. They told us the First Marine Division and the Army's Seventh Infantry Division had already been evacuated and the Army's Third Infantry Division was holding the defense perimeter. But, they said, the enemy was closing the gap quickly. We knew the situation was critical because thousands of refugees were crammed onto the beach for as far as we could see."

The colonels told LaRue they could not order him to take on any refugees, especially since his ship was equipped to handle only twelve passengers in addition to its officers and crew. "We can't order you to take them" one of the colonels said, "but we ask if you would volunteer to take your ship in and take some of those refugees off the beach. We ask you to confer with your officers and decide."

Lunney remembers that LaRue didn't hesitate. "He neither turned to his left or right, nor conferred with anyone. He responded that he would take his ship in and take off as many refugees as he could."

None of the ship's officers questioned their captain's decision or suggested a brief discussion among themselves before answering the colonels. And no officer cautioned that maybe they should just turn the ship around and get out of there, especially with all that jet fuel still on board.

"There was no concern about our individual safety," Lunney said. "Maybe it sounds corny, but we were doing our job. We were not scared. When the captain said we would take the ship in, we did it. We did what we were supposed to do."

*   *   *   *   *

Merl Smith remembers a moment of comic relief. An officer came on board later to coordinate arrangements to begin taking the refugees from the beach. "We knew we had more and better food than he had seen in a long time," Smith said, "so we offered to give him something good to eat—anything he wanted. I thought he'd ask for a nice, juicy steak."

The officer fooled Smith. He said, "I want an onion. I've been thinking about an onion for weeks." Smith said, laughing, "I couldn't believe it. An onion. He ate it like an apple, right there in front of us. I'll never forget that."

It was going to be a packed house aboard the *Meredith Victory* regardless of how many refugees came aboard. In the first few years after the evacuation, articles describing the feat said the ship had accommodations for only twelve passengers, but it is more accurate to say there were no accommodations at all for passengers. Engineer Merl Smith explained, "There were accom-

modations only for our thirty-five crew members and our twelve
officers," he said. "We had *space* for twelve other people, but not
accommodations. We didn't have twelve extra beds or twelve
extra anything. We just had room for twelve people, but the
space was not equipped."

After her captain's command decision, the *Meredith Victory*
moved toward the beach and tied up at dock number three,
next to another American freighter, the SS *Norcuba.* The Army
engineers quickly constructed a causeway that ran over the top
of the *Norcuba* to the *Meredith Victory* for the refugees to reach
the ship that was their only lifeline. "As far as the eye could see,"
Smith remembered, "there were refugees all over the place. All
you could see was people. It was a crazy scene." They began to
scramble up the side of the ship using cargo nets that the crew
had lowered over the side as stepladders.

Lunney added, "Those people had lived under the harsh rule of
Communism for five years, and they were voting with their
feet." Smith seconded Lunney's statement, adding, "They were
scared to death of the Communists."

Forty-nine years later, the same opinion was expressed by
Joseph R. Owen, a young Marine lieutenant in the war, a sur-
vivor of the Chosin Reservoir withdrawal, and the author of the
Naval Institute's book *Colder Than Hell.* In March 1999, at a conference sponsored by the Robert R. McCormick Tribune
Foundation and the U.S. Naval Institute, Owen said of the
refugees at Hungnam, "If that was their participation in a civil
war, they showed what side they were on with their feet. They
did not leave their homes and come out at the point of a bayo-
net." He added, "It made me realize that we were doing the right
thing in Korea, and I'm proud to have been a part of it."

Captain LaRue, who had carried cargo on the deadly Murmansk
run during World War II, turned to his ship's first mate, Dino

Savastio, and said, "Start them aboard. And let me know when the count reaches ten thousand." Lunney recalls, "The refugees were loaded like cargo. They were placed in every cargo hold and between decks. We had no food or water for them. No doctors. No interpreters. The temperature was well below freezing, but the holds were not heated or lighted. There were no sanitary facilities for them. They brought all their earthly possessions with them—children carried children, mothers breast-fed their babies with another child strapped to their backs, old men carried children together with whatever food they had saved. I saw terror in their faces. They responded meekly as we called out to them, '*Bali! Bali!*' That is Korean for 'Hurry! Hurry!' It was one of the few words we knew in the Korean language."

One of the Navy's most fabled officers of the twentieth century, Admiral Arleigh Burke, was at Hungnam then. In later years, he said, "I remember the thousands of woebegone Koreans who were hungry, destitute, and fearful, but who at the same time had that strong desire for freedom and the willingness to make sacrifices for freedom."

As the evacuation continued and the refugees poured across that makeshift causeway, most of the American military had been pulled out and the city was aflame from enemy gunfire. In retaliation, American warships were firing back, including the USS *Missouri*, where MacArthur had signed the surrender documents with the Japanese five years earlier. With its sixteen-inch guns, the *Missouri* was rattling the deck of the *Meredith Victory*, and Captain LaRue grew concerned that some of the friendly fire from the American ships might fall short. The noise from the *Missouri*'s guns was so loud that the ship's radio operator went to his bunk and refused to get up because he was scared.

There was no time to worry about that, though. A reporter asked Bob Lunney in later years if he cried at that point. Lunney said, "I found it such an absurd question I didn't know how to answer it."

Navy planes from three American carriers were dropping napalm bombs—a new kind of bomb that destroyed its target and then ignited a ring of fire around it.

For Lunney, in the midst of all that fierce wartime action, there was a touch of nostalgia, if that's possible in the heat of combat. The firepower was coming from two heavy cruisers, the *Rochester* and the *St. Paul,* as well as the battleship *Missouri,* three aircraft carriers, and anywhere from three to eight destroyers.

One of those carriers whose planes dropped napalm bombs on the buildings and facilities of Hungnam below was the USS *Leyte,* on which Lunney had served in the Atlantic with the Naval Reserve the year before. Most of the officers on the *Meredith Victory* were Naval Reserve officers. At its peak, Fast Carrier Force Seventy-Seven employed four attack carriers, one battleship, two cruisers, and twenty-two destroyers in covering the final phase of the evacuation of the X Corps from Hungnam.

At the same time, the Chinese were coming closer by the hour. The perimeter, which the Third Division was defending against increasing odds, was shrinking rapidly. Among those with a firsthand view of the action, with their lives hanging in the balance, were the members of the First Mobile Army Surgical Hospital—First M*A*S*H—the first medical unit sent into the war from the United States. In an abandoned school on the north edge of Hungnam sixteen doctors, thirteen nurses, and eighty-seven enlisted men with one jeep and fourteen World War II trucks operated a sixty-bed hospital where the surgeons could perform "meatball surgery." M*A*S*H units were something new, an attempt to provide immediate medical help to the wounded and keep them alive long enough to be transferred to better facilities and equipment in Japan and elsewhere.

The M*A*S*H personnel could see the action along the Hungnam beach as the Seventh and Third Infantry Divisions valiantly held the defensive perimeter against the advancing Chinese Army. The commander of the M*A*S*H unit, Lieutenant Colonel Carl T. Dubuy, later wrote, "From our hill immediately behind the school . . . we could watch the shells bursting between us and the tiny figures of the Chinese troops and their miniature horses moving about on the frozen plains between us and Hamhung. It was necessary to use a great deal of our precious supply of adhesive tape to keep the blast and shock of the constant bombardment from jarring out all the glass and letting in the cold through the school windows."

The booming sixteen-inch shells from the USS *Missouri* prompted Dubuy to describe the battleship as "that basso profundo." He said, "We were all convinced that they were actually shooting thirty-two-gallon GI cans since the projectiles sounded to us like garbage cans hurtling through the frozen air overhead."

Dubuy remembered later that many of the members of his unit were convinced that they "would never really escape in the evacuation of Hungnam. Certainly the atmosphere of constant bombardment, the overcast skies, the hustle and bustle of loading the troops and material on to the impatiently waiting ships, together with the word that the First M*A*S*H would be the last to leave, if and when, were all less than conducive to elevation of morale."

But they did leave, on a World War II liberty ship, the *Maria Lukenbach*. Dubuy's description of the ship sounds remarkably similar to the facilities and conditions on the *Meredith Victory*: "There were no quarters or personnel spaces on this type of freighter except for the ship's crew . . . No heat, no baths, indeed no water, no toilets, no beds in that drafty barnlike space dark as pitch. Sleeping bags were placed on the steel planking and the only heat was body heat augmented by togetherness. Latrines for us troops were rigged astern on the weather deck protruding outboard from the edges. Use of these facilities was an adventure in survival, requiring an iron grip on a rail during all operations while the exposure insured rapid turnover of the clientele, keeping the waiting lines short."

On the *Meredith Victory,* as Lunney and his fellow officers and crewmembers began taking on the refugees, he remembers, "There was a ring of fire around Hungnam. We were almost on the front lines."

While his men worked feverishly to take on as many of those refugees as humanly possible in the face of mounting pressure from the enemy, Captain LaRue took two precautions. He ordered the *Meredith Victory* to be turned around, so she would face the open sea in case she had to make a hasty withdrawal from shore. And he ordered his crew to keep her engines running throughout the loading operation.

"If the North Koreans and Chinese had broken through," Lunney said, "we would have fled. We were not going to surrender the ship."

The harsh North Korean winter added to the severity of the conditions. Winds reached gale force at times and it was snowing. The challenge of communications between the units on the beach was compounded when a fire destroyed the radio and cable section at Hungnam and ruined most of the equipment.

The first refugees to board the ship were guided to the fifth hold, five levels below the deck. Crewmembers lowered them using pallets usually intended to lower and lift cargo. The ship's log tells the story of the loading in the simple, matter-of-fact language of such logs. Entries beginning the evening of Friday,

22nd December 1950, show that the loading of the refugees began at 9:30 that night, continued all night, and was not completed until 11:10 the next morning:

> 2130 Commence loading refugees in #5 hold via platform . . .

> 2200 Commence loading refugees in #4 . . . using platform and jumbo gear . . . Hatches #1, #2 and #3 being loaded via ladders.

> 2315 Start loading #2 and #3 with platforms of refugees.

> 2400 Continue loading all five holds with refugees. Lights and lines check. Rounds made. All secure on deck.

> *—H. J. B. Smith Jr. 3/0*

Just before the *Meredith Victory* headed out to sea with her human cargo, a jeep came racing down the dock. A young Army lieutenant jumped out and dashed up the gangway and onto the bridge. He hurriedly told Captain LaRue, "The CID [Criminal Investigation Division] just received a tip that there may be some Communists aboard disguised as refugees. I have been detailed to accompany you to Pusan with an armed guard . . . I have seventeen South Korean MPs [military police] with me."

As the 22nd of December turned into the 23rd, the weather was "overcast and cloudy," according to the ship's log, with calm seas. The *Meredith Victory* remained on the port side of the *Norcuba* as the loading of the refugees continued. Floodlights were used to penetrate the midnight darkness, aiding the boarding but, as Captain LaRue remembered later, those floodlights made the dangerous situation even worse.

"Despite all the obvious risks, all our lights were switched on while we prepared to load. We were sitting ducks, perfectly outlined in the glare, yet no enemy shell struck even close. One of our own heavy guns could easily have lobbed a shell into the crush of people by mistake. Yet none did."

One officer described the scene with a vivid comparison that would be familiar even to small children. "It's crazy," he said. "It's like that joke the clowns play in the circus, where a dozen giants get into one tiny car."

Through it all, Captain LaRue was nervously aware that below decks with the refugees he was still carrying tons of jet fuel. In later years he put the total amount at three hundred tons. "A spark," he said, "could turn the ship into a funeral pyre," igniting the worst sea disaster in history. The danger was compounded by a severe lack of equipment—no lifeboats or life preservers for the refugees, only two boats and forty-seven life preservers for the forty-seven officers and crewmembers. Once out of the harbor they would be alone on the high seas with no radio contact because security was so tight. They would also be without mine detection equipment as they sailed back through that thirty-mile web of sea mines. The officers on the *Meredith Victory* knew what the refugees did not—that three Navy minesweepers were sunk by enemy mines in the two months before the evacuation of Hungnam.

Enemy submarines were suspected of operating in the area and could sink the makeshift rescue vessel with one well-aimed torpedo. The ship had no means of resisting an enemy attack from either the sea or the air. And once underway, she would have no escort ships.

Lunney, a veteran of World War II, described the situation as "an amphibious operation in reverse, with no precedent in military history."

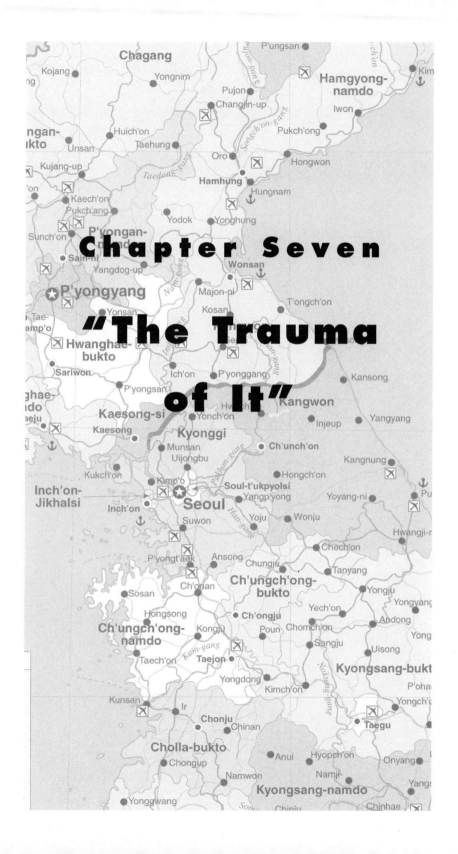

Chapter Seven

"The Trauma of It"

The Korean War was the first to be fought by a combined force made up of soldiers from countries belonging to the United Nations. Twenty-two countries participated. Here a wounded Canadian soldier is helped by one of his buddies.

The SS *Meredith Victory* alongside the dock at Pusan. Notice the antiaircraft gun emplacement with gunners on watch in the foreground. *Photo courtesy of J. Robert Lunney.*

Explosions caused by a United Nations' demolition team blowing up equipment and installations along the beach at Hungnam to keep them from being used by the enemy. The USS *Begor* lies at anchor. *Photo Courtesy of the U.S. Naval Historical Center.*

A group of U.S. Marines taking a break. These troops marched in subzero temperatures and through snow-covered mountains toward evacuation in Hungnam harbor during their dramatic escape from the Chosin Reservoir.

A bugler sounds "Taps" over the graves of fallen Leathernecks during memorial services at the First Marine Division cemetery at Hungnam, following the division's breakout from the Chosin Reservoir.

Only two years after President Truman ordered the desegregation of the armed forces, African American troops were included among the American GIs who fought in Korea. This soldier peers from his bunker while waiting with his machine gun for the "volunteer" Chinese Army.

Generous American GIs gained a reputation for their acts of kindness toward children caught in the hostilities. Above, we see Korean children enjoying a donated *Roy Rogers* magazine (as well as a pair of miniature cowboy boots). On the right, the *Meredith Victory*'s third mate (Al Franzon) is seen doling out chewing gum. *Right photo by J. Robert Lunney, courtesy of Al Franzon.*

After surviving the twelve-day ordeal from the Chosin Reservoir (the longest withdrawal in American history), a group of Marines climbs aboard a Navy transport ship for evacuation to South Korea.

General Douglas MacArthur watches the invasion of Inchon from the deck of the USS *Mt. McKinley*, September 15, 1950. This brilliant military maneuver, masterminded by the general, dramatically reversed the course of the war—although only briefly.

President Truman and General MacArthur meet on Wake Island on October 15, 1950. In a colossal misjudgment, MacArthur told Truman that the Chinese would not enter the war and that he would "have the boys home by Christmas." The Chinese entered the war only days later and may in fact have been in North Korea when Truman and MacArthur met.

Four U.S. LSTs unload men and equipment on the beach during the invasion of Inchon.

North Korean refugees on the road to Hungnam. Fleeing their homes, they brought only the possessions they could carry on their backs or pile onto carts pulled by people or oxen.

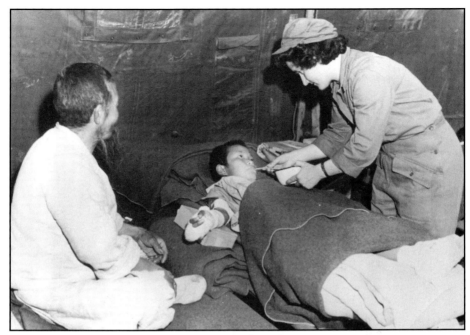

Children are always the innocent victims of war. Here an American nurse treats a thirteen-year-old boy at a M*A*S*H unit while his grateful father watches.

The refugees packed themselves onto any available vessel, including these fishing boats in Hungnam harbor. The sea was the only remaining escape route from the rapidly approaching Communist forces.

Pictured here are some of the 98,100 refugees who were rescued by American ships, (including this Navy LST and the *Meredith Victory*), and evacuated from Hungnam. *Photo courtesy of the National Archives.*

The main deck of the *Meredith Victory* packed with refugees. The refugees were even more crowded together on the three decks below the main, where this photo was taken.

The aft deck of the *Meredith Victory*, packed from rail to rail with refugees. This is only a small fraction of the fourteen thousand North Korean men, women, and children rescued by the *Meredith Victory. Photo courtesy of Al Franzon.*

Another view of the main deck. *Photo courtesy of J. Robert Lunney.*

General Mark Clark signs the truce documents at Panmunjom, Korea, on July 27, 1953. Two other members of the U.S. Armistice Commission, Vice Admirals Robert Briscoe (center) and J. J. Clark (no relation to the general), watch the peace-giving signature.

Almost ten years after the rescue, the hero of the *Meredith Victory*, former Captain Leonard LaRue of Philadelphia (left), receives the Merchant Marine Service Medal on August 24, 1960. Presenting the medal is Secretary of Commerce Frederick Mueller, representing President Eisenhower.

G eneral Haig's memory of the evacuation of Hungnam remains clear. "They all got out," he told me in April 2000. "It was an extremely traumatic time. We had enough firepower both onshore and offshore and enough air power that we could have stayed there forever, extracting massive casualties from the enemy. But the decision was made that we were going to get out, and there were a lot of good reasons for that in the strategic sense. You couldn't just sit there." Then Haig described his most lasting impression. "The trauma of it was in watching these refugees in that bitter, bitter cold standing in water up to their waist in some cases, waiting for someone to pick them up."

The young captain had come down from General Almond's headquarters in Hamhung in a jeep with Almond's communications van, radios, security equipment, and a jeep escort, all of them items for which he was directly responsible. All of the equipment was essential for Almond to operate as the commander of the X Corps in the field.

Haig said the decision to evacuate the refugees, even though they were the people of the enemy, was made all the way up the chain of command. "Almond weighed in at GHQ [General Headquarters, MacArthur's office in Tokyo]," Haig remembered, "and GHQ weighed in at Washington to make this withdrawal part of the evacuation. There was a lot of pressure against it, fearing that the delay would be dangerous. But, as always with micromanaging from afar, you have to listen to the guys on the ground. And they did, to their everlasting glory."

The future four-star general continued, "I watched it up to almost the end. I was one of the last out, on a freighter with Almond's equipment—his communications, his jeep, and other pieces. It was an orderly withdrawal, without crisis. The decision was made by MacArthur or his headquarters, I'm sure. And I'm sure they notified Washington that they had assembled enough ships to be able to do it. That was the big problem."

* * * * *

Simply surviving was going to be a problem for the refugees. In the biting Korean cold of December, many of the refugees had fled in their bare feet. Some wore only light clothing. Others wrapped themselves in newspapers.

They kept on coming. Merl Smith said, "You stood there and asked yourself, 'How many thousands are behind these? When are we ever going to end this job?'"

The entries in the ship's log for December 23 show that the end was not yet in sight:

> 0000 Continue loading Korean refugees at all hatches . . .
>
> 0330 Finished loading refugees in #2 and #5.
>
> *—A. Franzon, 3/0*

0400-0800 Overcast sky. Good visibility. Vessel loading refugees as before at #1, #3 and #4 hatches.

0500 Finished loading #4 hatch.

0700 Finished loading #1 hatch.

—*A. W. Golembeski, 2/0*

1110 Complete loading refugees. All GIs leave vessel.

—*H. J. B. Smith Jr., 3/0*

By the time the officers and crew finished "loading refugees," there were fourteen thousand of them on the *Meredith Victory*. Seventeen of the passengers had been wounded or injured. Five of the women were only days, maybe hours, away from giving birth.

Captain LaRue wrote later, "It was impossible, and yet they were there. There *couldn't* be that much room—yet there was." It was the morning of December 23. Pusan, their safe haven, was 450 sea miles away.

Colonel Appleman, a veteran of the war, wrote about the speeded-up efforts to accommodate as many refugees as humanly possible on the LSTs and merchant freighters like the *Meredith Victory*. In *Escaping the Trap*, Appleman said, "Those who saw the thousands of refugees jammed and packed into the LSTs that carried many of them south, exposed on open decks to freezing weather for three or four days, did not forget the sight. These refugees had to be desperate to take such physical torment and punishment. It was part of the war and should be recorded as such."

*   *   *   *   *

On the same day, the biggest story back in America was that General Motors had put its 1951 cars on sale again after a four-day freeze. Under pressure from the federal government, General Motors followed a similar action by Ford, agreeing to roll back its prices to the 1950 level. Now people could buy new Chevrolets, Pontiacs, and Cadillacs again.

The Associated Press' dispatch out of Korea that day said, "Quiet prevailed in the northeast after American forces smashed back the strongest Chinese and Korean Red attack thus far on the shrunken Hungnam beachhead . . .

"Hungnam beachhead defenses repulsed the Reds' most menacing assault thus far. After the battle, the hillsides were strewn with frozen bodies of Chinese and North Koreans garbed in white civilian robes."

The First Marine Division sailed from Hungnam for Pusan on December 15. The South Korean troops of I Corps were taken off the beach by ship on December 18. The U.S. Army's Seventh Infantry Division left on December 21. The Third Infantry Division arrived on the beach the next day after fighting a "blocking action" to allow the Marines to pull through the Third Infantry on their way to Hungnam. During the operation, which began on December 5, the Third Infantry was assigned to protect the rear of the Marines' column on their withdrawal to the beach. The Third Infantry arrived on the beach on December 22, after the Marines had sailed. The Third was the last Allied fighting force to join the perimeter on the beach and the last to leave.

Leo Meyer was a thirty-three-year-old member of the Third Infantry at Hungnam. He remembers that the fighting on the beach could have been a lot worse by the time his unit arrived on December 22, saying the Third "had little contact" with the enemy from then until they sailed on Christmas Eve afternoon. "I believe the Chinese commanders realized our intent," he said in May 2000. "Their mission was to get us out of North Korea. Since we were doing so voluntarily, why should they lose men in pursuit? So after the 22nd, they did not press hard."

In a detailed letter describing the situation on the beach from his unit's arrival on December 22 until the evacuation was completed on Christmas Eve, Meyer included this interesting insight into some unique competition among the American soldiers: "As an indicator of enemy action, U.S. troops wanted the honor of being the last man off the Hungnam Beach. Everybody wanted to be 'rear-end Charlie.' The Division wisely ordered each infantry regiment to evacuate the beach at the same time. Each one sent equal size units out to the ships. Battalion size, then company size and last, each regiment had one platoon on the beach that left together for their respective ships to rejoin their parent units. Therefore, no one regiment could claim to be the last off."

With the *Meredith Victory* and other ships carrying refugees already at sea, the Third Infantry was unaware that it was part of the dramatic story of saving nearly one hundred thousand civilians by holding "Line Charlie" as the civilian evacuation was completed. Meyer said, "We didn't realize we were saving North Korean civilians, for we saw none. We were survivors."

He remembers the conditions, the departure from the beach, and then the luxuries aboard ship—the shower, the clean clothes, the Christmas meal.

Meyer had one quick reaction just after being picked up: he gained new respect for his father. "We waded into the surf hip-deep and onto boats about 11:30 hours [11:30 in the morning], 24 December. The memories remain of the wet parkas, packs, carbines, and side arms." Then, Meyer recalled, "I realized how smart my father was when he advised me to join the Navy, not the Army."

Meyer was so overjoyed, he said, "I was in shock. As we were directed to our bunk area, we had to pass through the mess deck. The tables were set for Christmas Eve dinner. Table cloths, china, and Navy flatware. But above all, I remember—*I remember*—salad trays with celery, carrots, and olives! This after we had been eating out of tin cans since 17 November."

The memories continued to come back to him. "I found my bunk," he went on, "dumped my pack and weapons and headed for the ship's store. They would only sell me two sets of T-shirts and undershorts (understandably). Headed for the shower, did my thing, and went up on deck and threw my 'long johns' over the side. They got up and walked around." He said it was November 17 when he put them on and he had not taken them off until December 24. "No sweat," he added quickly, "we were all in the same boat, so to speak, and with the temperature being what it was, no one had a body odor."

The trip south to safety? "The voyage south was a luxury for three days."

Meyer, who also saw action in the Pacific during World War II and for the third time as a member of the Special Forces in Vietnam, said, "I wrote home (everyone did) on the ship en route from Hungnam to Pusan: 'Don't pay attention to the newspapers—I'm okay.'"

* * * * *

John Middlemas, now retired, was a decorated soldier in World War II, Korea, and Vietnam. He served as a warrant officer in the

Third Infantry Division at Hungnam. He was a member of "an under-strength rifle company"—Company A. It was the company's dangerous mission to man the point, the early-warning position responsible for spotting an enemy unit and engaging it in combat to prevent further penetration. Company A was one thousand yards in front of the Americans' defensive perimeter at Hungnam after a bloody two months following the entry of the Chinese into the war. The outfit was composed of sixty-seven American troops and two hundred "ROKs"—members of the Army of the Republic of Korea, South Korea's Army.

Middlemas said South Korea built up its numbers in a hurry by simply grabbing every able-bodied man its officers saw. "They would cut off a section of a town," he remembered, "and grab everybody." These rawest recruits would be given a haircut and a few clothes, a minimal amount of training, and would then be sent right into battle. "One man," Middlemas said, "left the house one day to get some medication for his wife, and she didn't see him for a year."

From mid-October to mid-December Company A suffered heavy losses during the first fiery battles with the Chinese and in the withdrawal to the sea that followed. By the time the company reached the perimeter around Hungnam on December 22, its strength had been reduced to 90 men, a loss of 177 killed or wounded.

Middlemas said the biggest potential challenge his outfit faced was a report from Air Force pilots who told them they had spotted ten thousand Mongolian soldiers on horseback in a large forest beyond the defensive perimeter outside Hungnam.

Middlemas said that whatever the precise number might have been, "It was a hell of a lot of Chinese." Fortunately, Company A never made contact with them. Its heaviest fighting along the

Hungnam perimeter came in "minor firefights" against the Chinese by roving patrols from Company A on the night of December 23, the night before the Third Division evacuated.

Most of the company's incidents occurred when units of the North Korean Army probed the American lines. "Foot patrols tried to make their way within our lines," Middlemas said. "But we had outposts. Without them, the enemy would have continued to probe until they met resistance from us. And if they didn't meet resistance, they would have continued until they met some. I think they would have started moving their main body closer." Middlemas said the mortar fire from Chinese units was "sporadic but furious, mostly at night."

Middlemas said, "We had no idea how close the enemy was." But his unit had a clear idea of why they were there. With the combat troops having already evacuated, the Third Infantry Division's mission was to protect the refugees as they continued to push and shove their way in terror onto the American ships waiting for them in the harbor. By the time the division was evacuated, Middlemas said, "All the refugees were gone. The only thing left was what we were blowing up."

I asked Middlemas the same question I asked others: Did the troops defending the beach and the sailors loading the refugees onto their ships object to exposing themselves to enemy fire while saving the lives of the people of the enemy? His answer was the same as General Haig's and others', and just as emphatic. "No," he said. "I don't think we harbored any ill will at all. We had a lot of discipline. We weren't rebels. We received orders and we carried them out. When orders came down, nobody would say, 'Let's have a town meeting on this.' You don't have time for that. If an order came down, that's it. You don't stand around thinking, 'Is there a better way to run up the side of this hill?' while some son of a gun is shooting at you."

Then Middlemas, who should know, added, "We did a better job than they did in Saigon."

Middlemas speculates that the Chinese limited their contact with the Americans in the last few days of the evacuation because the troops of the Third Infantry Division held their defensive positions so effectively. "They might have come if they had found a weakness in our line," he says today. Like others, he feels the Chinese reduced their level of contact and fighting in those final days of the evacuation because "they had already accomplished their mission"—the Americans were leaving North Korea.

Middlemas's memory of the voyage out of Hungnam is as clear as his ability to describe the action on the beach, which preceded the withdrawal. He verified Leo Meyer's account of the conditions they had endured. "When we got ready to shower on board ship," Middlemas said, "we saw that our hands and faces were black, but the rest of our body was lily white. We hadn't taken our clothes off in a month." He said he still thinks of those days when he puts on clean underwear and socks.

Four months after the Hungnam evacuation, Middlemas found himself back in combat, under fire, in a fierce spring offensive launched by the Red Chinese. He was wounded and later received a battlefield commission as a second lieutenant for bravery. He continued to make the Army his career and retired as a major.

A few years ago, his seventeen-year-old granddaughter asked Middlemas about his role in Korea. She asked him, "Grandfather, did you ever kill anyone?"

Middlemas answered, "I got ten awards for valor, so I guess I did."

"Isn't that gross! How could you ever have done something like that?"

Her grandfather had an answer. "Well, would you prefer that your mother have a dead father?"

The schoolgirl persisted. "But you really didn't have to do that, did you?"

"No," he agreed, "but then the other guy didn't have the best of intentions for me, either."

*   *   *   *   *

Thanks to the heroism of X Corps, under the command of Major General Edward M. Almond, and Naval Task Force Seventy-Seven under Rear Admiral E. C. Ewen, the evacuation of Hungnam, a stark yet shining page in human history, was complete.

In his 1992 book *Miracle in Korea,* Glenn C. Cowart wrote:

> To those who lived through the ordeal with its numbing cold, windswept ridges, lack of food and sleep and, above all, the constant specter of death or captivity, the Hungnam evacuation was, indeed, a miracle of the first magnitude.

The total number of people and amount of equipment evacuated demonstrates the enormity of the operation:

> 105,000 United Nations and South Korean troops
> 98,100 North Korean civilians
> 17,500 vehicles
> 350,000 tons of cargo

General Matthew B. Ridgway was the new commander of the Eighth Army at Hungnam. Four months later he succeeded MacArthur (after Truman fired MacArthur) and still later rose to become the Army chief of staff. In his book *The Korean War*, Ridgway said, "To take out 105,000 troops, 91,000 refugees [most sources put the figure at 98,100], more than 17,000 vehicles, and several hundred thousand tons of cargo was in itself a military triumph of no small dimensions."

After the evacuation was completed, members of the Tenth Engineer Battalion and the Navy underwater demolition teams, supported by a high-speed transport ship, the USS *Begor,* moved in to the beach to destroy all equipment and materials so they could not be used by the Chinese Communists or the North Koreans. Several boats evacuating American troops were overturned when the succession of blasts whipped up waves and leveled the Hungnam waterfront.

While the *Missouri* supported the demolition team by firing 162 rounds from its booming sixteen-inch guns, the Americans exploded four hundred tons of dynamite, detonated five hundred one-thousand-pound bombs, and torched two hundred drums of gasoline. Despite the force of all that firepower, everything was not destroyed. Navy destroyers were sent in as close to the beach as they could get to fire directly into the stacks and piles of equipment and ammunition.

During their action on the beach the men of the Third Division fired more than forty-six thousand rounds of ammunition, while the Navy did its part by launching more than twelve thousand shells at the beach.

The U.N. military personnel who had been on the beach were gone. The refugees who had been on the beach were gone. Now the beach was gone, too.

*   *   *   *   *

The Third Infantry Division reported that loading the 100,000 troops was complicated because of the 98,100 refugees. "They pressed against docks and loading areas hoping for rescue from the oncoming Communists," the report said. "They stood in masses, their worldly possessions strapped to their backs, children clutching at the hands of their parents, hunger, fear and despair etched deeply in the faces of all. Civil Assistance Teams had done what they could to alleviate their suffering, but the only real cure for their wretchedness was to be taken away from this land in which they had been born, but which had become a place of evil. Their plea for help could not be denied."

As for the final defenders of the beach at Hungnam, the courageous men of the Third Infantry Division, their story has been largely overshadowed by other tales of heroism. The Army report described their overnight growth from boys to men, from green recruits to battle-hardened veterans, from care-free kids to young men who were growing up the hard way and could now take their place proudly with those who had gone before them in the two world wars:

> They were only a few weeks away from the scenes of home, but it seemed like a thousand years. Then, most of them had been recruits. Now they were veterans. They had fought their fight and knew they would fight again, but it wouldn't be something strange and unknown next time. Now, there were heroes among them and others who no longer answered roll call. A part of the mass of humanity covering the decks was the Koreans who had joined the Division at Beppu. They had shared the rations, the dangers, the small comforts. They too had buried their dead and they too had their heroes . . . They

were all successors of the men who'd been at Anzio,
on the Marne and in the Siegfried Line.

The shoes of the old-timers were well filled.

These men had deeds of their own to remember.

Captain LaRue said he could not understand the remarkable accomplishment of cramming fourteen thousand refugees onto his small freighter, even as he saw it happen. "Somehow, somewhere," he said, "eight thousand tons of steel were stretched to make room for all who came."

Bob Lunney remembered that most officers, except those whose duties required them to try to squeeze their way onto the deck from time to time, "never knew what the Koreans were doing. We couldn't communicate with them. And they were very quiet, even stoic. They were mostly peasants—farmers. They hoped they were headed for a better life, but they didn't know. They had crammed themselves onto our ship in their desperation to get away not just from the Chinese troops who were trying to catch them to kill them; they were also desperate to get away from the harsh and dictatorial life which had been forced on them by the Communist government of their own country, North Korea."

One of the most serious concerns of the officers on board the *Meredith Victory* was keeping the refugees' families together. As they boarded, the officers segregated refugees by gender. But the officers soon realized they were breaking up every family and, with the crowded conditions, the families might be broken up forever. Even after they allowed families to remain together, the officers wondered how many of them would be broken up anyhow, with some members already separated because of the segregation practiced at the start of the loading. If they reached Pusan safely, the refugees in the upper holds and on deck would leave the ship first, and it would take hours before those in the lower holds, who had boarded first, would be able to come to the deck and leave. By that time, the rest of the fourteen thousand would have been taken off the ship. Who could tell where they would be? "We wondered how they could ever meet each other again," Merl Smith said. To this day, no one knows how many families were broken up forever by the fortunes of war on that rescue voyage.

As the ship sailed, Captain LaRue remained in cool command. "He had a bright, clear mind," Staff Officer Lunney said, "and with that mind, he chose to do what was right, good, and just without being encumbered by questions. I always thought if he lost his ship, his officers, and his men, and those fourteen thousand refugees, he would have felt he did the right thing."

LaRue's officers never questioned his leadership or his decisions. "And we never discussed the pros and cons of war or why we were there," Lunney said. "We were just doing our job. We knew we were helping to protect a sovereign nation—South Korea. And we knew the United States was committed to protect their interests versus Communist aggression, which was a major concern in the world at that time. We always felt we were doing the right thing."

General Haig agrees. When asked if he felt the evacuation was worth the risk they were taking, he didn't hesitate. "I never had any doubts about the wisdom of the decision to evacuate the refugees," he answered with emphasis. "It was my feeling that it was a human issue of unparalleled proportions. These poor people—hell, if we believed in *anything*, it was getting them out. That was never an issue with me. I was a very strong advocate for doing it. I wasn't a decision maker, but occasionally I got in a word or two."

As for the risk factor, Lunney said, "I felt very confident that everything necessary would be done to achieve this rescue.

There never was any concern of mine that we might fail." Lunney based his confidence on the knowledge that the ship had experienced senior officers and crewmembers and effective leadership. "Our captain, our chief engineer, our chief mate, our engineer officers, and our other senior officers all were veterans of World War II," he said. "The Chinese had only numbers. We controlled the sea and the air. I never had any concern about our getting out."

Smith expressed the same attitude. "We felt we were invincible because of World War II," he said.

In their confidence, Lunney and Smith were able to joke about what could happen to them and the disturbing possibility that they might be captured. Lunney told one of the ship's cooks, Wong Win, who was Chinese himself, "It won't be any problem for us. We'll be treated like officers and gentlemen—except you."

Lunney and Smith remembered that all of the officers and members of the crew, including Captain LaRue, were impressed by the conduct of the refugees, despite their desperate plight. Lunney said, "He was touched by it. We all were."

Even after providing a lifesaving escape for fourteen thousand human beings, the officers and men of the ship thought the United States should be doing even more. Merl Smith said, "We thought we should chase the Communists into Manchuria [the Chinese province adjacent to North Korea]."

Did they agree with MacArthur in his desire to extend the war into China? "I thought MacArthur was right in wanting to go into Manchuria," Smith said, "but I thought he should have made that argument behind closed doors. And eventually he should have just obeyed President Truman and followed the orders of his commander-in-chief."

Lunney said they never feared the grim specter of World War III, which was the subject of widespread public discussion back home and in other nations around the world. "I called home before we left for Korea," he said, "and the biggest concern of my parents was whether I would miss the opening of law school at Cornell in September. But all of us thought I would be gone for only a short while."

They had a reason for feeling that way. "We reminded ourselves that we were Americans," Lunney said. "We had just won World War II. North Korea was going to be a pushover. There was never any concern about our winning this war or being successful. There was no concern about support back home. There was no negative feedback."

* * * * *

On a normal voyage, the officers would have spent their spare time in the "saloon" playing chess, but occupying their off-duty hours was not much of a problem on this voyage because they were standing watch four hours on and eight off. In between watches, most of the time was spent simply getting some sleep—"sack time" in military jargon.

Their quarters were located on an island in the center of the ship near the front. They had to keep the refugees out, so officers secured their quarters from the inside. The only way to get in was from the bridge, where those operating the ship guided it, maintained its course and speed, and kept on the lookout for anything suspicious that might be a potential threat. If the officers on the bridge wanted to go onto the deck, they had to struggle their way through the refugees to get there.

Merl Smith was in his quarters when he heard a tapping on the porthole of his tiny room. When it continued, "I opened it," he said, "and hands and arms came shooting through there. They looked like spaghetti hanging over the porthole into my room. I gave them water, which they craved in their thirst, but I couldn't satisfy them. Some other officers had to come into my room and help me close the porthole."

For the rest of the voyage, Smith and his fellow officers kept the "dead light," a metal cover for their portholes, closed. "I never again let any of the refugees see into my room," he said. "It caused a panic. But I still don't know how they survived that voyage without water for three days."

The refugees were desperate in every way. Ashley Halsey Jr. described their desperation in his *Saturday Evening Post* article the next year. "The fatalities could have been enormous. Panic, cold, exhaustion, people falling numbly over the side, sudden epidemic—anything could have happened during the three memorable days of the voyage."

As for the shortage of food, Halsey wrote, "One ragged refugee, standing near the ship's galley, got his hands on a hard-boiled egg. He swallowed it, shell and all, before anyone could take it from him. Others, given oranges by the pitying crew, bolted them with the skins still on."

The North Koreans had to control their stress as well as their physical trials. "They never showed any fear," Lunney says, "and we never saw any expression of fear on any of their faces. We had no toilet facilities for them, and the smell was overpowering. By the time we reached Japan after our rescue, the entire ship had to be washed down. When we got back to the States and docked at Seattle, the longshoremen couldn't believe the odor. And that was a month later. It was still that strong."

*   *   *   *   *

Among the North Koreans aboard the *Meredith Victory* as she steamed out of Hungnam harbor were a twenty-nine-year-old mother named Lee Keum-Soon (Magdalena) and her three children—an eight-year-old daughter named Kang Soon-Hwa (Maria), a six-year-old son named Kang Soon-il (Andre), and an infant son named Anton, who was then eight months old.

The family had left their hometown of Hamhung, a half-hour from Hungnam, on a truck in November. At my request young Anton, who grew up to become Father Anton Kang, a Benedictine monk in Seoul, asked his mother, now seventy-nine years old, about her memories of their lifesaving voyage.

She told her son that she and the other North Koreans were "terribly afraid" of being persecuted by the Communists, "especially since they were Catholics." The Communists knew that the Catholics opposed them and their mistreatment of citizens. His mother said, "Life after 1945 was really very hard . . . they mistreated people, especially Catholics."

Father Anton learned from his mother that "they were very much scared." When the refugees finally headed for Hungnam, "the roads were full of refugees."

Father Anton, who is the director of the Benedict Retreat Center in Seoul, said his mother told him that his father worked for the Communist government before the war. "Since he was Catholic," Father Kang said, his father "was all the time under suspicion." Father Kang added, "Just before the Korean War, he was actually sentenced to death in secret, but one of his fellow men let him know it, so he eventually escaped to the mountains for hiding about three or four months."

Father Kang's mother remembers that the family was unable to bring any possessions at all from their home to Hungnam because their house "was exploded by bombs." As they huddled later in the cramped conditions in one of the *Meredith Victory's* below decks, Father Anton said, "My mother was very much afraid of our safety . . . My mother was so scared of the whole proceedings she doesn't remember the exact situation which was going on at the time." His mother told him that she and her other two children "talked to each other during the voyage about their uncertain future and the remaining families and relatives . . . They prayed vehemently every day and night on the ship."

*   *   *   *   *

Early in the voyage, Captain LaRue asked Bob Lunney to check out reports that the refugees were building fires on some of those hundreds of drums of jet fuel so they could stay warm and cook what meager supplies of food a few of them had. Lunney investigated and found the reports were true. Some of the refugees were burning fires on top of the drums, creating the very real possibility of larger fires and explosions that could have killed everyone on board. Instead of becoming history's greatest sea rescue, the voyage could have exploded into history's worst sea disaster and caused fourteen thousand people to perish.

With Lunney unable to speak Korean and the Koreans unable to speak English, he was forced to rely on hand signals and the universally understood word, "No." He waved his hands and arms vigorously and repeated rapidly, "No! No! No!" Then he and his fellow officers quickly doused the fires. The refugees understood. They built no more fires.

Rumors, one of the most serious problems in any war, surfaced several times during the voyage. Word spread among the passengers that the Americans were going to take the *Meredith Victory* out into the open sea and drop an atomic bomb on it. The officers suspected that the ridiculous story might have been spread by one of those spies that the Army lieutenant warned them about just before they sailed out of Hungnam.

Another rumor was that some of the refugees elsewhere on the ship had already died. Still another, maybe more believable to the desperate refugees, was that the Americans were going to take the ship away from land and dump the refugees overboard.

"Those poor people," Merl Smith said, "had to be thinking the world was coming to an end."

The seventeen Korean MPs were fed in the crew's mess room. On the second day at sea, the chief steward noticed during breakfast that he had served eighteen meals to the MPs instead of seventeen. A check revealed that a North Korean Communist spy had come aboard with the MPs, dressed in a South Korean uniform. He was stripped of his uniform and shackled to a post for the rest of the voyage.

The threat of riots hung in the air every hour of the day and night. The danger became critical late in the voyage when a few younger Korean men made a move on the crew's quarters—off limits to the refugees—apparently fearing that the *Meredith Victory* could not get them to Pusan. The ship's officers and the Korean military police somehow were able to reassure the youths that they were only a few hours from Pusan and safety.

Captain LaRue later wondered in chilling terms, "What would have happened if fourteen thousand persons, jammed into one small ship, had suddenly become maddened by terror? I doubt that the vessel itself could have survived . . . Many of us were white-faced as we listened to the rumble of that menacing mob."

LaRue said the riot never occurred because, "without knowing the language, the ship's officers and men somehow made the frightened and angry refugees understand that safety was now only a few hours away."

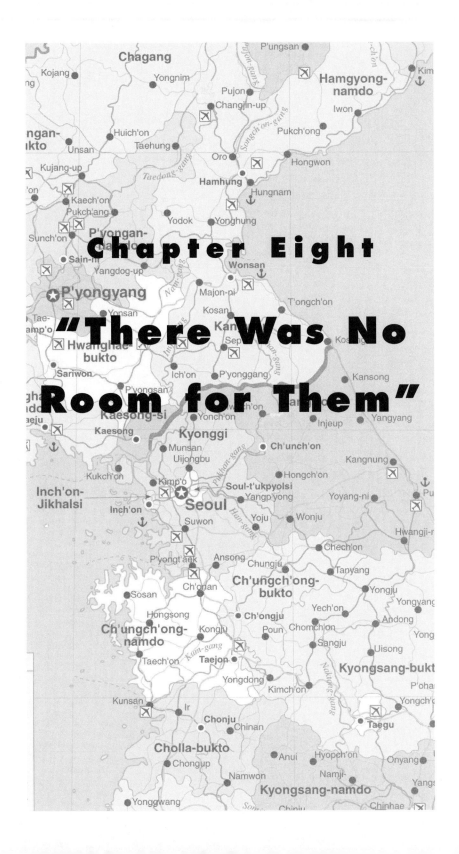

Chapter Eight

"There Was No Room for Them"

O n their first night on the Sea of Japan, the ship's first mate, Dino Savastio, shouted up to Captain LaRue on the bridge, "Hey, Captain! How many you figure we got on board?"

The captain hollered back down to the deck, "You know the count—fourteen thousand."

Savastio shouted back, "Well, Captain, it's 14,001 now!"

A baby had been born. Bob Lunney was summoned to the infirmary, a small room with a double-decker bunk, water, and not much else.

"As I tried to assist," he told me, "I began to realize the other Korean women around this woman were going to be able to deliver the baby on their own as midwives. Korean women considered childbirth a natural event. They didn't know anything about prenatal care or the need for doctors. They were used to working in the rice fields, having their babies right there in the fields, and then going right back to work. We thought this was a major event, having a baby amid those conditions, but to the Korean women, including the mother, it was no big deal."

Lunney stood by, ready if needed, and watched the delivery of a healthy baby boy in the midst of the most dramatic sea rescue in the history of the world and in the middle of a full-scale war. Amazingly enough—but not to the Korean women—four more babies were born during the rest of the voyage.

"As soon as we saw the women taking over at each birth, we stepped aside and just stood by in case we were needed. We made sure the women were comfortable during and after each birth, and we gave them towels and hot water," Lunney said. "They breast fed their babies, so nature took care of that need."

Lunney saw smiles all around, but there were no shouts of joy. The mothers in each case "just checked the hands and feet and wanted to hold their babies, but otherwise they went about life naturally and without any great concern."

The members of the crew? "They were smiling and happy too," Lunney said.

Savastio wrote home to his family, "There I stood with babies all around and something doing every minute."

The crew members named the firstborn "Kimchi" after a hot and spicy all-natural dish popular in Korea, made with cabbage, red pepper, garlic, salted fish, and ginger, then fermented for at least four weeks in clay containers.

The men of the *Meredith Victory* are confident that the baby's mother later gave him a real name.

*   *   *   *   *

Maybe the cruelest blow of all came on Christmas Eve, when the *Meredith Victory* pulled into Pusan at long last, only to be told she could not dock there. The city was already overloaded with thousands of refugees. When officials pulled alongside his ship, Captain LaRue told them, "I've got fourteen thousand refugees. Where do I put them?"

He said he was stunned by their reply. They said, "Not here." More than one million refugees were already in Pusan, overtaxing its space and facilities.

LaRue was jolted by the news and fearful of the reaction by the refugees when they learned their journey was going to take longer. "Could you imagine," he speculated, "the fright of our refugees when they realized there was more of the nightmare voyage yet to come?"

The captain was told to head his ship to Koje-Do, an island about fifty miles southwest of Pusan, where the flood of refugees was now being received. Merl Smith remembers, "That was a heartbreaking development for those poor refugees."

Before pulling up his anchor, Captain LaRue "was determined to get some help for my people. It took hours of slicing through red tape, but we finally managed to get food, water, and some blankets and clothing from our own military supplies in Pusan. I also got a few interpreters and military police to make the last leg of the journey with us."

Captain LaRue remembered that heartbreak a few years later when he expressed his own reaction in moving, biblical terms:

> The message of Christmas, the message of kindness and good will, had come to this woe-laden ship, to these people aboard who, like the Holy Family many centuries before, were themselves refugees from a tyrannical force. I thought as I watched, "There was no room for them, no room in their native land."

The ship's log shows that loading the additional provisions and the extra personnel was a major undertaking. It took seven and a half hours:

> 0000 Commence bringing rice aboard and feeding Korean refugees in hatches and on deck.
>
> 0730 Completed feeding refugees.

> *—A. W. Golembeski*

Captain LaRue remembered another sight that evening, as his requests for rice and other provisions were being fulfilled and the interpreters and military police were boarding. It dawned on him that this was Christmas Eve. The night had arrived, with its bone-chilling temperatures and clear sea sky. The refugees were being fed and the interpreters were calming their fears. Then LaRue noticed something else. Members of his crew were passing among the refugees and giving away their own extra clothing.

As the *Meredith Victory* steamed toward the beach at Koje-Do, Raymond Fosse, the captain of a transport, the *Sgt. Truman Kimbro,* tried to make out exactly what he and his fellow officers were seeing. In an article for *The Skipper* almost ten years later, Captain Fosse told writer Edward F. Oliver, "When we first saw that victory ship, we couldn't figure out what in the world it had on deck. From a distance, it was simply a dark, solid mass. As the ship came nearer, we could see it was human beings. And there wasn't a sound from them. They just stood there, silently, waiting. Unless you saw it, you couldn't believe it."

The next challenge for Captain LaRue and his ship of miracles was the topography of their landing point. The harbor was small and crowded so the ship, its miracle workers, and their refugees had to remain in the open sea overnight.

Once near the beach the next day (Christmas), the men of the *Meredith Victory* faced yet another challenge—unloading the refugees. The ship was landing at a bare, empty island with no dock and no facilities to guide the freighter in to the beach. LSTs would have to finish the journey. The refugees were placed on square platforms, the kind used to raise and lower heavy equipment on and off a ship. The platforms held sixteen people at a time.

The sea heaved up and down, threatening to swallow any of the refugees at any moment as they carefully made their way down the side of the *Meredith Victory* on a platform and into the waiting LST. Engineer Al Kaufhold remembers seeing a seventy-year-old woman lose all of her earthly possessions, which fell over the side while she attempted to board the LST. He said the sight was heartbreaking because this woman, whose own life had been saved by the voyage from Hungnam, suddenly had nothing else in this world except her life.

Kaufhold also remembers a happier sight at nearly the same moment: a girl about seven years old standing on the deck of the *Meredith Victory* in bone-chilling cold with only light clothing on, but smiling the smile of a happy little girl. Why? Because even in her extreme discomfort, she knew as she watched the refugees in front of her being taken off the ship and onto the LST that she was almost safe.

*   *   *   *   *

All of the refugees were starving and terribly thirsty. As they sat at anchor in the outer harbor for the tedious and drawn-out unloading, there was no elbowing or pushing, no one threatening to jump overboard and swim to shore, no shouts of joy. Instead the refugees maintained their stoic behavior, that same silence and endurance that had long before won the admiration of all the officers and crew members on board.

Captain LaRue remembered the scene in an article for *This Week* magazine on December 11, 1960, two weeks before the tenth anniversary of the rescue: "And here, too, danger rode with us," he wrote. "The only way we could unload was with the aid of LSTs, large ships designed to land tanks on shores during combat. One after the other, two of these vessels drew alongside and again we went through a nerve-jangling ordeal. Each person had to climb the rail of the *Victory* and be lowered into the LST."

The captain remembered the grave risk of serious injury or even death. The two ships, each with a capacity for up to 8,500 passengers, were tied together so that the refugees could step from the freighter onto the LST, just above a swelling sea that caused the vessels to pitch perilously. The hull of the *Meredith Victory* kept banging against the hull of each LST as it loaded more refugees from the freighter. "The lines might part," LaRue feared. "Somebody could be crushed between the two ships."

He said refugees flocked to the side of the freighter "from every nook and cranny." Fathers untied their sashes and retied them around the waists of their children, then lifted them from the ship's holds onto the deck.

"Koreans do not show emotion readily," he wrote, "but as I stood on the bridge, I saw expressions on faces that, even now, bring a warm glow to my heart. Our passengers, waving gaily, gave us all glances of profound gratitude."

An account of the miraculous voyage by James Finan, published in *Naval Affairs* and later in *Reader's Digest*, estimated the number of refugees at fifteen thousand. Finan said officials in the shipping industry apparently did not believe the figure could actually be that high and presumably blamed it on a typographical error, so they marked the number down to 1,500 in their printed accounts.

The ship's log for December 26 reflects the completion of history's largest rescue from the sea:

> 0915 Commence transferring refugees to LST.
>
> 1200 Refugees continue moving into LSTs, M.P.s on duty about vessel.
>
> —*H. J. B. Smith Jr.*
>
> 1200–1600 Weather fine and clear. Visibility very good. Light to gentle NW'ly breeze. Continue disembarking Korean refugees into LST Q636 and LST BM 8501, Army M.P.s and ship's crew assisting.
>
> 1320 LST Q636 away full loaded.
>
> 1445 Finished disembarking Korean refugees. Vessel searched and all refugees found departed.
>
> 1455 LST BM 8501 away . . .
>
> —*A. Franzon*

Charles Regal, a columnist for the *Seattle Post-Intelligencer*, measured the magnitude of the *Meredith Victory*'s accomplishment. He wrote, "That surely was the largest number of persons ever taken aboard a freighter, any size, and it may be the largest load ever taken by any ship." He pointed out that "the enormous *Queen Mary*," built to accommodate large numbers of passengers as a large ocean liner, averaged between two and ten thousand troops during her transatlantic voyages after being converted to a troop ship in World War II.

Regal may have been the first reporter to tell the story of the *Meredith Victory*. As soon as the ship docked in Seattle, a month after the rescue at Hungnam, Regal wrote, "The amazing story of a mass evacuation of 14,000 Korean civilians in one over-flowing shipload out of Hungnam December 22 was disclosed in Seattle Monday upon return of the SS *Meredith Victory*."

He reported that Navy Captain M. E. Eaton, commander of the Military Sea Transportation Service, said the evacuation "probably is an all-time world's record for one ship." Regal said Eaton called it "a fine, humanitarian act" and a "credit to the American Merchant Marine and the United Nations."

Bob Lunney told me he credits the refugees themselves with a major role in their own rescue. He said, "Each of us took away some part of Korea in our own hearts and souls because of the stoicism and bravery of these Korean people. I still marvel at them."

Staff Officer Lunney remembers that Captain LaRue's demeanor continued unchanged throughout the voyage and as they pulled into Koje-Do. "He remained unmoved," Lunney said. "He was still giving orders and running that ship." Lunney attributed the success of their massive rescue to the captain's makeup. "He always saw things in a bright, clear line, with nothing encumbering him," Lunney said. "He never looked left or right. There were never any distractions. He asked not one question. For him, the whole issue of whether to try to rescue that many people was an easy decision. He behaved exactly the way you or I would under normal circumstances. We succeeded because of his faith and his motivation. He knew that even if the whole ship blew up and every one of us was killed, he would still be able to stand before his Maker some day and say, 'I did the right thing.'"

Lunney also said LaRue held up even better than the rest. "He was a man of iron," Lunney said. "He was solid, stable, responsible—in command at all times."

*　　*　　*　　*　　*

At Koje-Do on Christmas day, both Merl Smith and Bob Lunney wrote letters to the folks back home. As they did, their families were reading headlines in *The New York Times* that morning that read:

EVACUATION OF HUNGNAM IS COMPLETED; CHINA REDS CROSS PARALLEL FOR DRIVE; SEOUL IS BEING CLEARED OF CIVILIANS

Subheads below those headlines told the readers that the lives of 205,000 men, women, and children had been saved—105,000 American troops and 100,000 North Korean refugees. Above the headlines was a reminder of the season:

TODAY IS CHRISTMAS! DO NOT FORGET THE NEEDIEST!

The Washington Post also made the evacuation of Hungnam its top story on that Christmas morning, although the refugees were not mentioned. Below were two bulletins, one saying that the Defense Department had announced the evacuation was over, the other saying President Rhee had advised all nonessential government workers to leave Seoul. The Korean National Assembly was "moving immediately to a southeast Korea port."

Also on page one was a picture of President Truman pushing a button in his hometown of Independence, Missouri, to light the national Christmas tree on the White House lawn at 5:16 P.M. on Christmas Eve.

An Associated Press dispatch described the final hours of the evacuation:

> In the tiny Hungnam beachhead, only remaining Allied position in northeast Korea, an orderly withdrawal continued. The Reds poured mortar shells into the area, but made no ground attacks. (This reference to the withdrawal was passed by the military censor in Tokyo, without elaboration.)

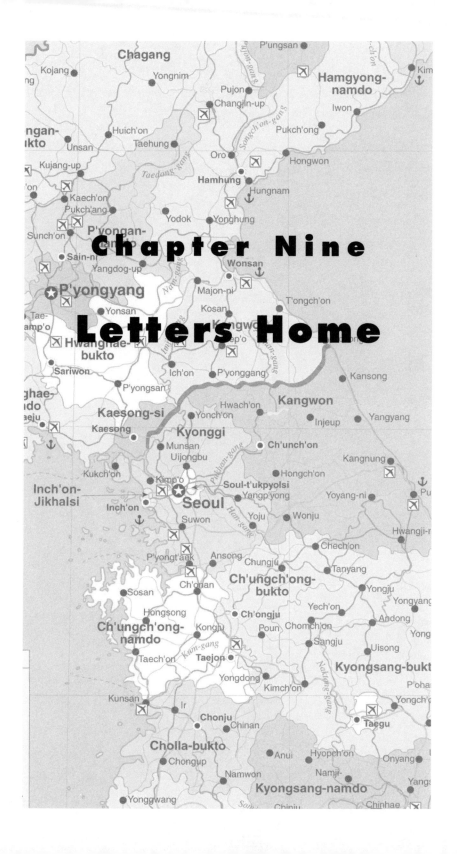

Chapter Nine

Letters Home

While Americans everywhere rejoiced over the news from Hungnam, they were also enjoying the holiday offerings at the movies and on television. Red Skelton was starring in one of the holiday movies, *Watch the Birdie*, while Betty Hutton and Fred Astaire were tripping the light fantastic in *Let's Dance*. New York's legendary Radio City Music Hall was showing Rudyard Kipling's *Kim*, starring Errol Flynn. Newspaper ads said the landmark theater at Rockefeller Center was also featuring "The Music Hall's great Christmas Stage Show" with its "world-famed Yuletide pageant."

In 1950, Americans were still listening to the radio at home, and many of them did not even have radios in their cars. On its *U.S. Steel Hour*, NBC radio featured a production of "David Copperfield," starring Boris Karloff, Cyril Ritchard, and Richard Burton. An operatic tenor who also enjoyed popularity with the general public, Lauritz Melchoir, was starring in another NBC radio production, "Silent Night." The Mutual and CBS radio networks carried King George's annual Christmas message. On television, NBC featured "Hansel and Gretel" and another special, "One Hour in Wonderland" starring Walt Disney and two of his closest friends, Mickey Mouse and Donald Duck. Ventriloquist Edgar Bergen was also on the show, with his sidekick Charlie McCarthy dressed, as always, in tuxedo, top hat, and monocle.

The influence of the war was showing, even in what we were watching on TV and listening to on the radio. In a preview of the holiday programs, Wayne Oliver wrote in an Associated Press story, "The tenor of the programming will be in keeping with the seriousness of the international situation. A reminder— if one is needed—that the nation is in an undeclared war will come from programs on Christmas Day on two radio networks, during which GIs in Korea will talk with folks back home."

Merl Smith couldn't talk to the folks back home, and neither could Bob Lunney, so they wrote letters on Christmas day, in their first hours out of danger at Koje-Do island. Smith wrote:

> Dear Folks,
>
> This is a Xmas day I will never forget as long as I live. We went back to Hungnam as I knew we would after I wrote my last letter in Pusan. We were there three days and left the day before the soldiers were all sup- posed to leave. Our cargo from there is <u>14,000</u> [Smith's emphasis] refugees. We started loading them on the 22nd and left the morning of the 23rd. We are now waiting to unload them onto an LST which will take them ashore as there is no dock here or even a port. As you know, this ship is designed for only cargo. We have five holds and each one has three decks with no lights and no heat. They were put on wooden plat- forms and lowered into the holds. As each deck was filled, it was covered over and the next deck loaded. When all holds were filled, the hatches were closed and then the main deck was loaded so that it is a solid mass of people . . . They have no toilet facilities except the few containers we could find for them. In the holds there is room for them all to sit down if they draw up their knees. Even though it is cold, the smell on here almost makes you sick. You don't think any- thing of being away from home for Xmas when you see what these people are going through. Too bad

these people don't have a lot of relatives living in the U.S. like the people of Europe do. We carried tons of CARE packages to Germany once when those people were better off. I'll bet I never see that much done for these people. The people on deck are constantly begging for water but we only carry enough for 50 men. We have given them as much as could be spared but it's only a drop in the bucket. Just before leaving Hungnam a little girl was stepped on and killed. The father carried her ashore and was told he had one hour to bury her before we sailed. I don't know if he ever did get back in time . . . You can't blame the conditions here on the Army. They have sent 90,000 people out of Hungnam and each time a ship moves into the limited amount of dock space it means that much delay in loading the equipment. They claim they would have evacuated sooner if it weren't for all the refugees who want to leave.

While at Hungnam there was a ring of smoke and fire around the city. In the daytime the planes would strafe and bomb the "Reds." At night all the naval ships would start firing from the shore batteries. I don't see how the enemy had the nerve to keep attacking the place. They were a lot closer than when we were there the first time. Hope all the soldiers got out okay.

This is all for now. I'll mail this when we get to Pusan after leaving here.

Love to all,

Merl

P.S. It's now 2 P.M. here so it's midnite of the 24th there. Merry Xmas.

Lunney began his letter with a first-person description of the scene as his ship loaded the refugees on dock at Hungnam three days earlier:

> From our anchorage we could see all of the planes and naval attacks on the shortening perimeter. The first rocket ships in the area sailed right past us to get into position for a rocket attack. At night all you could hear were the five and eight-inch guns plus the rockets being fired into the Chinese lines. During the heaviest part of the firing, I got out of the rack and made for my door and only realized what happened when the cold air hit me and I woke up. Luckily, all the firing was from our guns, and there was no harbor attack by the Reds while we were there.
>
> We went into the docks Friday nite, the 22nd; the harbor was then packed with approximately fifty ships (both merchant and naval) . . . The original plan was to fill our lower holds with cargo, then take about a thousand troops on top of the cargo. Upon arriving at the pier, where we tied up with another ship, we got the word that we were to load North Korean refugees: 10,401, and this did not count babies on their mothers' and fathers' backs which seemed to be between three and four thousand more, making a final total of refugees about 14,000. They were instructed to bring food and water (whatever the poor people could scrape together is beyond me, for the whole dock area was completely leveled). In the meantime, an intense naval and air barrage was going on. The perimeter was two miles in depth now. So we were within two miles of the front lines. Naval shells kept flying over our heads and bursting in the near distance, and one could see the planes on their diving runs spurting rockets and

machine gun fire. The military constructed a wooden ladder and causeway over the other ship right to us, and the people piled on by the thousands.

It was now dusk and you could see the lineup of people as far as you could look. Old people, maimed, on crutches, kids still nursing at their mother's breast, old men with children strapped to their backs; eighteen came aboard in litters, expectant mothers, carrying crying children.

It was truly a pitiful sight . . . In the sick bay one mother had already given birth . . . The people were all fed in Pusan by the military who came aboard about eighteen strong, including some South Korean M.P.s. One poor fellow cut his foot badly and had to be put ashore in Pusan, and as we sailed he was still crying to have his wife put ashore with him.

I just wonder how many homes this mass evacuation has broken up. They just all had to be evacuated or be killed by the Reds for cooperating with the Americans. There were 30,000 in all, and it took three Victory ships to load them. We originally got orders to take them to Pusan but received diversion orders while under way for Koje-Do (an island just to the S.W. of Pusan), but as luck would have it, the message never came thru, so into Pusan Christmas Eve with the poor lot . . . Now I realize that the people on deck are the lucky ones, for the people are packed together so tightly in the lower holds that they cannot move, much less get fresh air. They are packed just like sardines. No toilet facilities and no water or food, much less an occasional change of air thru the ventilators rigged for cargo—but never a human cargo.

The decks are just littered with filth and human feces. The whole ship just stinks to high heaven and you cannot turn without meeting the odor. Just imagine a city of 15,000 people jammed together on this ship without facilities to handle them and the dirt and disease that will ensue.

We are now anchored off Koje-Do and awaiting LSTs to come alongside to remove them . . . They have been aboard now seventy-two hours and even if they start discharging immediately it will take twenty-four hours to get them all off.

Never have I felt the want to be home as I have this Christmas. With all this death and destruction looking you in the face everywhere, you turn with a feeling of utter helplessness; one just feels that he has had enough of war. I just imagined and read of the heartrending sights of modern war, but this exposure has given me my fill. I have gone out on deck and walked around, looking at the people, all huddled together, trying to keep warm, mothers with babies clutched tightly and fathers trying to keep their sons warm under their own coats, and one cannot help but swell up emotionally and cry. I have given all my chocolate out and the ship has given them water as best they can, while the crew gives out as much food as is permissible, but as is true in all these cases, 14,000 people cannot all be fed and watered . . .

As it was, we got out of Hungnam in the nick of time with the people because it was all evacuated within twenty-four hours after we left, and at least we have saved them from the hands of the Communists. You can imagine what it must be to live under Communist rule, if all these people who have lived under it for five years are willing to endure this to get away from them.

Our Christmas dinner was fine, and I know that Mother prepared a good one for all of you back home, and don't think I wouldn't have liked to have been there. This reminds me of a sentence I read in the Steward's cookbook which the boys will appreciate—"'when do we eat?' Thru out the years this loud and lusty call of the 'inner man' has been a challenge and an inspiration to good cooks everywhere" . . . Mother, please take note.

A postscript dated December 28 in Pusan brought the folks even more up-to-date:

Did not have a chance to send my last letter till now, so this postscript. Anchored off Pusan the 26th, after discharging refugees into two LSTs, within six hours (much faster than we had all expected) off an island where I think all 91,000 evacuated from Hungnam were dumped. We came into the pier at Pusan this morning and are trying to clean up the vessel. I don't think we will be too successful, for what we really need is a fumigation. They are busily engaged in discharging the rest of our cargo (jet fuel) now and will be finished within the next two days.

The latest is that we go to Sasebo, Japan, from here. For what, I don't know. It is only about ten hours from Pusan, so it may be for another war cargo for Korea.

About now all the fellows are wanting to go home and I don't blame them . . . But hopes for going home or staying do no good with the military running things. Ship's agents just came aboard with 600 bucks for advance to the crew, so must sign off and have them mail this for me (and besides, I have to get to work, doling out the dough).

Love to all,

Bob

As Smith and Lunney wrote their Christmas letters, a radio dispatch from Seoul described Christmas day there: "This war-ravaged capital, its civilian population bewildered by Communist aggression, went ahead today with plans to celebrate the birth of Christ. Nearly all churches have planned Christmas day services. It will be a brief Christmas for most of the people. Many are cold, their homes piles of rubble covered by a thin mantle of snow."

The radio dispatch continued, "In past years, churches had streamers across their doorways which read 'Celebrating the Holy Birth of Jesus.' It is the Korean way of saying, 'Merry Christmas.' Although the city is threatened with a second Communist invasion within six months, Protestant and Catholic churches expect many worshippers Christmas day."

A second radio dispatch sounded more ominous: "Elements of Chinese and North Korean Communist Armies, more than a half-million strong, massed along the 38th parallel Saturday for an imminently expected offensive against the U.S. forces in Korea." The report continued, "General Douglas MacArthur announced that four additional Chinese Armies are reported to have entered North Korea recently to augment an estimated 260,000 regrouped North Koreans threatening a Christmas offensive against the United Nations."

In the midst of such mixed messages, Truman, MacArthur, Army Chief of Staff J. Lawton Collins, and Vice Admiral C. Turner Joy—the commander of Naval forces in the Far East—sent Christmas greetings to the American fighting men in Korea. Admiral Joy, who later headed the team that negotiated the truce ending the war almost three years later, may have said it best:

> On this particular Christmas in the Far East, when peace on earth and good will among men are so fervently sought and so rarely found, it may be necessary for us to probe deeper than at any time in the past to understand the true meaning of that day.

Chapter Ten

Kim Jung Hee's
Fifty-Year Search

"I believe God sailed with us those three days," Captain LaRue later wrote in *News Digest*. "I believe this because by all the laws of logic, the loss of life could have been enormous. Yet not a soul perished. Time after time, dangers that threatened to explode into disaster were miraculously averted."

Former Lieutenant Bob Lunney is quick to credit the Navy for its role in the Hungnam evacuation. "We couldn't have done it without the Navy," he says today.

The Navy returned the compliment in the form of a message of congratulations from Admiral Joy to the Merchant Marines:

> My most sincere congratulations on a job well done. Your performance throughout the Korean campaign has always been notable. In the successful redeployment of ground forces from northeast Korea your initiative and your enthusiastic and prompt response to all demands indicate that your organization is at its best when the chips are down. The merchant mariners who performed for you did so silently but their accomplishment speaks loudly. I find it comforting to work with such teammates.

The Army in turn praised the Navy. General Ridgway was lavish in lauding the Navy for its achievements in making it all possible in the first place. "The Navy at Hungnam," he said, "performed with spectacular skill, although they received no banner headlines for their evacuation by sea of the entire X Corps and its equipment. But to take out from unfriendly territory 105,000 troops, 91,000 Korean refugees, more than 17,000 vehicles, and several hundred thousand tons of cargo was in itself a military triumph of no small dimensions. Equipment and supplies that could not be outloaded were destroyed on the beach, so nothing was left to the enemy."

Military historian and author Shelby L. Stanton agrees. "The success of the evacuation was primarily a Navy triumph," he wrote in his book, *America's Tenth Legion: X Corps in Korea, 1950.* "Without warships and merchant vessels," he said, "the greater portion of X Corps would have been annihilated in an overland march."

Stanton also quotes a passage from the Army's history of the war: "Fortunately, and for reasons best known to themselves, the Chinese made no concerted effort to overrun the beachhead, although light scattered thrusts suggesting reconnaissance in preparation for larger operations were made by them throughout the evacuation operation."

Most authorities agree that approximately 98,100 North Korean men, women, and children were saved from their own Army and the loud public threats of their supposed ally, the Army of Communist China. Estimates at the time said the number equaled the entire population of Emporia, Kansas, or Salisbury, Maryland. Some observers compared the achievement to carrying that many people aboard a rescue ship with no accommodations all the way from Baltimore to Jacksonville, Florida.

Because of the wartime conditions that surrounded the *Meredith Victory* and threatened her safety every inch of the way and every minute of those three days, Staff Officer Lunney described it in still more dramatic terms: "Never in recorded history have combatants rescued so many civilians from enemy territory in the midst of battle."

Lunney showed his emotions in an interview on a video program called "Korean War: The Untold Story," hosted by actress Loretta Swit, who played Major "Hot Lips" Houlihan in the hit television series *M*A*S*H*: "The experience that moves me so much when I recall the Korean War is to remember the women, and the children, and the babies. Their only access to safety was the sea, and my captain chose to take every last one of them off that beach."

When they arrived at Koje-Do, there was no speech by Captain LaRue to his officers and members of his crew. Lunney explained, "He never thought it was extraordinary. His happiness was just that we were successful, not necessarily heroic or gallant. He just had a feeling of satisfaction, as we all did, that we had rescued these people and they would live in freedom. That was extremely important to everyone in those years, because there was a great fear of the growing communist influence throughout the world."

*   *   *   *   *

In his follow-up survey of twelve Hungnam survivors for the Eighth Army twenty-five years later, Stanley Bolin found that mere survival was still the overriding challenge facing the refugees as they attempted to begin a new life in a new country. Food was a basic problem, especially for those who had to live in the crowded refugee centers because they had no family members in South Korea. One of those interviewed said he was near starvation "many times."

Most of them needed at least several years to begin putting their lives back together after that awful December in 1950. Most of the twelve had lived in several towns and held more than one job while attempting to find a way of life, a home, a permanent job for themselves, and a better life for their families. Six of the refugees who were interviewed said they moved two or three times in that short span of time. One said he moved his family a half dozen times in those years.

They worked in a variety of jobs in their first twenty-five years in South Korea—as waiter, bartender, carpenter, accountant, hospital orderly, store clerk, at a pier, even as a vendor selling ice cream—anything to begin earning a living again. Others worked as day laborers at the American military bases. One worked as a medical assistant in a United Nations hospital. A refugee wife sold cigarettes on the black market to help feed her children. Several who had been farmers in North Korea began to farm unused wasteland near where they landed in South Korea. Still another one of those interviewed said it took him twenty years, until 1970, to achieve the financial stability to be able to buy a home.

Bolin's report identified the tenacity of the refugees, the same characteristic that so impressed the officers and crew of the *Meredith Victory,* as the part of their makeup that enabled them to literally save their own lives. Bolin wrote, "The twelve people interviewed—as well as other Hungnam evacuees that this researcher has come into contact with—appear to attack life's problems with an unyielding tenacity. Over the past quarter-century they have refused to allow their plight to overwhelm or to enervate them." He cited their attitude of *Ddosuni,* meaning "Never say die." He said most of the refugees remembered "that time when they were snatched from the jaws of death as a time of rebirth."

Bolin also cited an attitude that was common among the refugees, and still is today: "Ask any Hungnam evacuee and he (or she) will tell you that their story has another chapter yet to be written. A chapter in which their divided homeland will again be united and they in turn will be reunited with lost loved ones." Writing in 1975, Bolin said, "It is to this end that they, as a community, are building toward a strong future. It is to keep the flame of this dream alive that they call upon their fellow citizens in the Republic of Korea to celebrate this, their twenty-fifth year as a free people."

* * * * *

Lee Keum-Soon (Magdalena) and her three children, including the future Father Anton Kang, director of the Benedictine Retreat Center in Seoul, stayed on Koje-Do for a year. Then, reunited with her husband, the family headed toward his hometown of Taejeon City and later to Seoul, where he found work in his pre-war profession as a bank clerk.

During those years young Anton felt the calling to become a priest, originally as a parish priest but then changing his mind to become a Benedictine monk. When I asked him why he decided to became a priest he said, "I thought I had to do something different for the people . . . "

Over the years since the history-making events at Hungnam and aboard the *Meredith Victory*, no member of the family has ever returned to the North, even though other family members had to be left there in 1950. "We never knew what happened to them," Anton said.

* * * * *

Kim Jung Hee typifies the same characteristics that Bob Lunney and Stanley Bolin have recognized. The mother who continues to search for her missing husband and daughter since they were separated on the dock at Hungnam fifty years ago has spent large amounts of time and money in her cause.

She told her nephew, Peter Kemp, that their voyage to Pusan on an LST was "very terrible." She said it was severely cold and the ship was packed with refugees on the main deck and below. She said the American sailors were gracious enough to share their biscuits with some of the refugees. Sanitation did not exist. She said refugees who were able to do so squeezed their way to the side of the ship to go to the bathroom. All around, she said, people were sick, coughing, and throwing up from seasickness.

The young mother spent the journey from Hungnam in one of the lower holds below deck, where there was no ventilation, amid conditions much like those endured by the refugees who reached safety several days later aboard the *Meredith Victory*. She said crying babies added to the discomfort, but the babies had reasons to cry, including being covered in their own waste because their mothers had nothing with which to clean them.

At Pusan, Kim June Hee cleaned her two children and herself. The American soldiers set up a station to spray the arriving refugees with the chemical DDT to rid them of infections. This chemical has long since been banned in America and other nations for use on crops because it has been found to cause cancer. But at Pusan in 1950 no one knew the dangers, so the refugees were covered from head to foot with the white spray of DDT.

Kim June Hee recalls today that there was no camp for the refugees at Pusan nor any organized means of handling them, so many left for the hills on the outskirts of the city to scour the ground for materials from which they could build crude huts as their first homes in South Korea.

The young mother was confident she could find an aunt, her father's sister, who lived in Taegu, so she boarded a train from Pusan with her two children and traveled there. She did not have to worry about money to pay for the train tickets. Before leaving North Korea she had alertly taken gold, silver, and precious gems from their jewelry store—rings, earrings, hair pins—and wrapped them around her stomach in a secret belt. She had also hidden clothes for her baby inside her own clothing. She redeemed some of the gold for cash and bought her train tickets to a new life in Taegu. After only a few days she found her aunt—Major Kemp's grandmother—and lived with her for almost a year, then settled in Seoul. She sold all of her jewelry and opened a silk store, selling clothing and silk material.

Her nephew, Peter Kemp, remembers from his days of growing up in South Korea that his aunt did well in her silk store in Seoul and was able to use some of her financial resources to pay for her continuing search. In the 1970s, Peter was living with his aunt and his grandmother in Seoul. He said that she was doing well enough to afford a rare luxury in Korea—her own car. It was a Japanese car—not really a fancy one, but Kemp adds, "yet it *was* fancy, because no one else had one."

While she continued to succeed with her silk store, Kim June Hee traveled to other cities in South Korea to place newspaper ads asking for information about her missing family members. Meanwhile Peter and his mother immigrated to the United States in 1975, when he was sixteen. They settled in Arlington, Virginia, just outside Washington, D.C., where Peter graduated from high school. Then he joined the U.S. Army, completed Officers' Candidate School, and began an Army career. He went to night school at the University of Maryland and earned a degree in modern history.

Major Kemp recently told me that his aunt continues her search today, even though she has already spent so much time and money. "When China and South Korea began a dialogue in the 1980s," he said, "people started going back and forth. My aunt began placing ads in Chinese newspapers. She even paid two men who said they could find her husband and daughter. Both times she thought she was close to finding them. The men took her money, but she never saw them again."

Kim Jung Hee still sees her husband and daughter in her dreams. Major Kemp's mother, however, has told her, "When you see someone in your dreams, that's bad. That means they've gone to the other side of the river."

His aunt responds emphatically, "No. I know for sure they are still alive."

How does Major Kemp feel about his refugee aunt and her expensive, time-consuming, fifty-year search for her lost husband and daughter?

"She's my hero," he says.

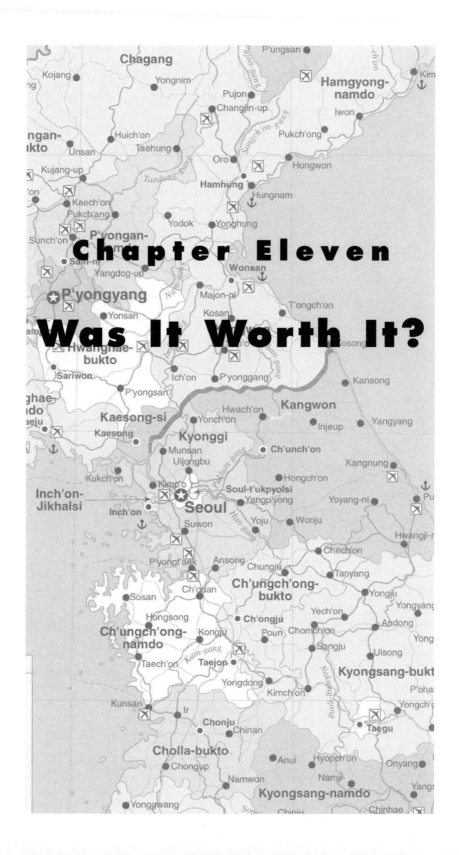

Chapter Eleven

Was It Worth It?

In North Korea, life is far different than the world south of the 38th parallel. Soon Park, the schoolgirl who fled from Hamhung to Hungnam while her mother tearfully returned to her husband and Soon's brother, went back to South Korea in 1979 and to North Korea in 1990. On her visit to North Korea, her former country, she traveled to Pyongyang and found it to be a city for "the chosen few." She described the North Korean capital city as "modern—clean, no pollution." But the rest of the country, she said, is "poor. Those people have nothing."

Soon Park was not allowed to visit her hometown of Hamhung.

She learned that the Communist government had killed her parents and her brother and that the citizens of North Korea "cannot say anything against their government." She jokingly called it a policy of "don't ask, don't tell." She said the people of North Korea cannot trust each other. She added that the citizens have been "brainwashed" by their government.

During her visit to North Korea, Soon, now an American citizen who earned a college degree and worked toward a master's degree before marrying and raising three children, spoke to her sister's son about relations between the two Koreas. All of the members of her family are now communists, she said, and her nephew boasted that North Korea could deliver an atomic bomb from Pyongyang to Washington "easily."

Soon laughed at his attitude and asked longingly, "Why do you not just embrace each other? After fifty years now, who is the winner?"

The United States, aware of North Korea's nuclear capability and its strong push to develop a delivery system for launching guided missiles armed with atomic warheads toward the United States, is in turn developing an X-band radar component as part of the United States National Missile Defense System, according to a report in *The Washington Post* in May 2000. The *Post* said the Defense Department has plans to build the radar defense on a remote spot in the Pacific Ocean, Shemya Island, where it would sit directly in the path of any missile fired by North Korea against the United States. The American Central Intelligence Agency reports that North Korea could develop an ICBM system in the next ten years.

*   *   *   *   *

Bob Lunney reported other observations about life in North Korea today. Lunney is now a retired rear admiral in the New York Naval Militia, the naval equivalent of a state's National Guard. In 1997 the North Korean government invited Lunney to be an observer at the third recovery of remains of American fighting men in North Korea. On his return, he wrote a three-page, single-spaced memorandum to his commander, Rear Admiral Robert A. Rosen, Commander of the Militia, reporting his observations not only about the operation of recovering the remains but also what he saw and observed about life in North Korea.

Lunney's memo, written on Veterans' Day, read in part, "On the third of our four days in the country we were given an escorted visit to the DMZ [Demilitarized Military Zone, the no-man's land separating the two countries]. Few have viewed this historic demarcation line from the North. We drove 100 miles south of Pyongyang on a 6-lane road named, ironically, the Reunification Highway, with its last exit sign, albeit inoperative, directing one to Seoul. We saw little of any North Korean preparations but the picture is deceptive. It is reported that their bunkers are well camouflaged with land mines strategically placed together with missile silos. We were sternly instructed by a senior colonel, NKPA [the North Korean Army], that the North Korean people believe that Americans are still the enemy and that if hostile relations by the U.S. government continue it will be difficult to normalize relations."

Lunney continued, "Our trip provided rare insights into a country where everyone wears a small metal badge with the face of the 'Great Leader,' Kim Il Sung [who died in 1994] on it surrounded by a color-coded rim indicating the wearer's position. There are no badges for his son, 'Dear Leader' Kim Jong Il, yet. Electricity is rationed and there are few vehicles around, except for trucks, mostly Army, some run on charcoal engines. Few bicycles are seen and no mechanical equipment is evident in the fields as all harvesting is done by hand. The streets are deserted at night."

Lunney found that "the food crisis is not as widespread as believed and does not affect the entire population. Distribution of food in this highly stratified nation benefits the Communist Party and its 1.1 million-man army but leaves regions suffering from famine and malnutrition. Despite its food problems the country still devotes substantial resources to erecting and maintaining grandiose statues, monuments and portraits of its leaders."

During his visit, Lunney said, "the rigidly controlled government television mostly shows stories of contented workers, loyal soldiers and extraordinary feats of Kim Il Sung. No foreign news broadcasts or publications are allowed. No advertising can be seen. The people are told they are ethnically superior and their country is the best in the world. No religion is allowed. The expectation of any change in North Korea was challenged by statements from the all-powerful Workers Party, which had just named Kim Jong Il as its leader on the eve of our arrival. There could be no wavering in its hard-line policies as announced by the official North Korean Central News Agency."

Lunney noted that "there are over 8,100 American servicemen still unaccounted for, and over 100 personnel allegedly in North Korean hands at the time of the truce in 1953. Despite our requests, no arrangements were made for us to meet with North Korean veterans or American military defectors."

*   *   *   *   *

The two Koreas have undergone role reversals in the almost five decades since the war ended with a truce on July 27, 1953. South Korea was a struggling nation during the 1950s and into recent years, while North Korea was propped up by assistance from the Soviet Union and China under orders from Stalin and Mao.

Today South Korea has become relatively prosperous while North Korea has struggled since the collapse of the Soviet Union in 1989. Reports from inside the harsh dictatorship indicate that conditions have worsened considerably in the North since Lunney wrote his report three years ago. They confirm that a full-fledged famine has gripped that Communist nation for the last three to five years, killing as many as two million citizens. Word leaking out of North Korea is that millions of people are surviving only by eating leaves and the roots of plants. Their homes are cold from lack of coal or heating fuel, and the factories where they once worked stand idle in the nation's paralyzed economy. The country's leader, Kim Jong Il, who succeeded his late father, Kim Il Sung, has become a recluse while his country staggers under the stark possibility of starvation and eventual collapse.

This grim picture is relieved to some extent by aid from the United States, but the North Korean dictatorship has intercepted even that. Correspondent John Pomfret of *The Washington Post* has reported that recent refugees have told him that food and medical supplies intended for children never get there. Instead, members of the Communist Party, military officers, and others loyal to the government grab them up. A French relief organization, Action Against Hunger, was refused permission to set up soup kitchens for North Korean children who had been abandoned by their parents and then denied admission to state-run nursery schools. Today they are living on the streets as they try to stay alive.

The United States General Accounting Office issued a report in October 1999 saying it could not determine whether American aid was reaching its intended recipients in North Korea because, among other reasons, North Korea had violated its signed agreement to submit accounting reports to the United Nations' World Food Program on a regular basis. One doctor told the *Post's* Pomfret that medicine was distributed on the basis of "ten per cent for war preparations, ten per cent for the people and eighty per cent for the officials."

Against this backdrop, the leaders of the two countries— President Kim Dae Jung of South Korea and Kim Jong Il, the ruler of North Korea—signed an agreement on June 14, 2000, in Pyongyang, to begin cooperative efforts toward reunification of the two nations on the split peninsula. Kim Dae Jung said signing the "historic agreement" ushered in "an era of conciliation and cooperation."

Koreans in both nations as well as people around the world are keeping their fingers crossed. There have been other agreements, signed in 1972 and 1991, but still no real progress toward reunification. Several key issues were unmentioned in the new agreement, including North Korea's emphasis on weapons development and the continued presence of thirty-seven thousand American troops in South Korea.

Richard Boucher, the State Department's spokesman, said "Our commitment to the security of South Korea is very, very strong." He added that the United States intends "to maintain peace and stability on the peninsula."

*   *   *   *   *

Captain LaRue, always a religious man, entered a Benedictine monastery, Saint Paul's Abbey in Newton, New Jersey, in 1954 after twenty-two years at sea and took the name of "Brother Marinus." He is still there today at age eighty-seven, confined to a wheelchair. The abbot at Saint Paul's, Father Joel, says Brother Marinus spends his time reading in his room and praying and sharing meals with his fellow monks. Contrary to what most people believe on hearing his religious name, he explained that it comes not from the Latin word for the sea but from Mary, "the Blessed Mother of God."

Brother Marinus still receives occasional visits from his staff officer on the *Meredith Victory,* Bob Lunney. During a Christmas visit there, Lunney asked Brother Marinus to explain to Lunney's young son, Alexander, how he was able to make his fateful decision to rescue the refugees off that beach at Hungnam in the face of such danger and at the risk of losing his men.

The monk turned and said softly and simply to the teenage boy, "The answer is there in the Holy Bible: 'Greater love hath no man than this, that a man lay down his life for his friends.'"

For all of his active years at St. Paul's, Brother Marinus operated the monastery's gift shop on the highway that leads to the abbey. Except for trips to the doctor, he has left the abbey only once in his forty-six years there. That was to be recognized for his bravery and leadership in special award ceremonies in Washington in 1960. Even for such a high honor, Brother Marinus did not want to leave the Abbey. He was at the ceremonies only because the abbot, the Right Rev. Charles Coriston, who delivered the invocation and benediction, ordered him there.

On August 24 of that year, almost ten years after he commanded his incredible rescue, some of Washington's highest dignitaries gathered at the National Press Club, where Secretary of State Dean Acheson ten years earlier had said that South Korea was not within the defense interests of the United States, to honor the ship and her captain. Four United States senators were in the blue-ribbon audience, as well as five members of the House of Representatives, two admirals, the Korean ambassador, and President Eisenhower's secretary of commerce, Frederick Mueller.

The ship was presented a plaque as a "Gallant Ship," and Brother Marinus was awarded a Meritorious Service Medal, the Merchant Marine's highest honor. Unit citations and ribbons were presented to Brother Marinus, his officers, and his crew.

The Gallant Ship award was authorized by a special act of Congress and signed by President Eisenhower. The award required a special act because the period for authorizing such an award had expired. In 1959 support for granting special authorization grew stronger. One of the powerful forces favoring the award was the Department of Defense and the Navy's chief of legislative liaison, Rear Admiral John S. McCain Jr., father of the current United States senator from Arizona, who was also a candidate for president in the year 2000.

In a letter to Herbert C. Bonner, chairman of the House Committee on Merchant Marine and Fisheries, Admiral McCain said, "It is believed that the issuance of a citation and award of a plaque to the Steamship *Meredith Victory* and the award of an appropriate citation ribbon bar to members of her crew, as this bill would provide, is an appropriate recognition of the outstanding feat performed by this ship in December, 1950."

Admiral Arleigh Burke, the young Navy officer who witnessed the fury and the miracle of Hungnam, had risen to the Navy's highest uniformed position, chief of naval operations, by then. At the awards ceremony he voiced high praise for the ship's officers and crew for their courage in saving the North Korean refugees. He said, "That these people might live in freedom, and that they might have hopes that their children could also live in freedom, required great effort and drastic measures by sympathetic men. The captain, the officers, and crew on the *Meredith Victory* were sympathetic men; they did take the required drastic measures; they were successful and, as a result of their extraordinary efforts, many people are now free who otherwise might well be under the Communist yoke. Many unknown Koreans owe the future freedom of their children to the efforts of these men whom you are honoring . . . "

The Maritime Administration's news release called the accomplishment of Brother Marinus and his men "the greatest rescue operation by a single ship in the history of mankind."

A memorandum accompanying the citations lists each member of the ship and his assignment, stating, "The attached Gallant Ship Unit Citation is to be awarded to the entire crew of the SS *Meredith Victory* as listed below." The memorandum then named all of those officers and crewmembers:

> Joseph Blesset, Wiper
> John P. Brady, Chief Engineer

Robert H. Clarke, Utility
Russell V. Claus, Messman
Richard C. Coley, Ordinary Seaman
Charles C. Crockett, Oiler
Sidney E. Deel, Assistant Electrician
Andres Diaz, Wiper
Alvar G. Franzon, Third Mate
Major M. Fuller, Steward
Lee Green, Fireman/Watertender
Nathaniel T. Green, Radio Officer
Albert W. Golembeski, Second Mate
Lawrence Hamaker Jr., Oiler
Edgar L. Hardon, Utility
Morall B. Harper, Electrician
Charles Harris, Able-Bodied Seaman
Leon L. Hayes, Utility
George E. Hirsimaki, First Assistant Engineer
Joseph A. Horton, Fireman/Watertender
Lonnie G. Hunter, Able-Bodied Seaman
William R. Jarrett, Able-Bodied Seaman
Kenneth E. Jones, Able-Bodied Seaman
Leon A. Katrobos Jr., Ordinary Seaman
Alfred W. Kaufhold, Licensed Junior Engineer
James A. Kelsey, Junior Third Assistant Engineer
Leonard P. LaRue, Master
J. Robert Lunney, Staff Officer
Herbert W. Lynch, Chief Cook
Patrick H. McDonald, Able-Bodied Seaman
Adrian L. McGregor, Messman
Ira D. Murphy, Deck Utility
Willie Newell, Assistant Cook
Vernice Newsome, Wiper
Nile H. Noble, Third Assistant Engineer
Elmer B. Osmund, Boson
Harding H. Petersen, Second Assistant Engineer
Johnnie Pritchard, Messman

Dino S. Savastio, Chief Mate
Henry J. B. Smith, Junior Third Mate
Merl Smith, Licensed Junior Engineer
Louis A. Sullivan, Fireman/Watertender
Ismall B. Tang, Ordinary Seaman
Noel R. Wilson, Able-Bodied Seaman
Wong T. Win, Second Cook and Baker
Ernest Wingrove, Deck Utility
Steve G. Xenos, Oiler

The remarks by Brother Marinus in accepting the Gallant Ship Award for his officers and crew provided an insight into his makeup—his faith in God, his modesty, his patriotism, and his all-around sincerity. In occasionally formal language, he said:

> One of the first maxims a man learns in going to sea is to always give another man a hand with a job he cannot do himself. The entire safety of the vessel and all that she carries depends on this principle. You might say that this is a corollary of "Thou shalt love they neighbor as thyself." In fulfillment of this principle at Hungnam, the cooperation and sustaining efforts of both officers and men, their devotion to ideals and duties as Americans and as seamen were outstanding and exemplary. In addition to the references made in this regard, I should like to add my own personal attestation, my commendation, and my gratitude for their endeavors. More than all this, however, our thanks are due to Divine Providence for the successful outcome of this venture.
>
> When the actual fighting had terminated in Korea in 1954, I entered St. Paul's Abbey as a candidate for the religious life. There was never a more emerald colored greenhorn than I! Sometimes I am asked what the dominating factor was in this metamorphosis. In

answering this inquiry, I like to recall three short lines from the writings of a Trappist, Father Raphael Simon. His words are brilliant in their simplicity and even more so in their meaning. I should like to pass them along to you—

To fall in love with God is the greatest of all romances.

To seek Him, the greatest adventure.

To find Him, the greatest human achievement.

It was not until I had crossed the threshold of the monastery that I discovered, amongst other things, that the particular Congregation of the Benedictine Order to which St. Paul's is a family member, in its various mission territories entrusted to its care, labored also in Northern Korea. There, some of the Benedictine Fathers and Brothers had been martyred at the hands of the Communists.

The evacuation from the beleaguered beachhead at Hungnam, of these freedom-loving, good neighbors of ours, the Korean people, was, in its broader aspects, truly a tragic incident in a tragic war. A war formulated by Communists, undertaken by Communists, waged by Communists, in their determination, which does not cease, to enslave *all* mankind! It should contain for us a moral of the *first* magnitude!

In answer to this diabolic evil which is Communism and to the other satanic forces that assail us both as a nation but even more so as individuals, let us ask God daily, in our own words, to give us the courage, to give us the backbone, to live fully and completely His ten commandments.

In returning to our monastic family at St. Paul's, both Father Abbot and I wish to assure you and the officers and men of the *Meredith Victory* and all your loved ones that you will not be forgotten in our prayers. We ask, in your charity, that you remember us in yours and especially remember all of the men of the sea; for theirs, in more than a physical sense, is both a trying and a hazardous calling.

In closing, the former master, officers, and men of the *Meredith Victory* wish to leave you with a seaman's greeting. This comes especially from the heart of a seaman turned Benedictine who wishes you and our country smooth sailing and always happy days.

Thank you, and may God bless you.

The awards to the ship and her men by the American government were not the first. Two years earlier President Syngman Rhee of South Korea issued a Presidential Unit Citation to the men of the *Meredith Victory*. The citation said in part:

The arrival of the *Meredith Victory* in Pusan after a three-day voyage through dangerous waters was a memorable occasion for all who participated in this humanitarian mission and is remembered by the people of Korea as an inspiring example of Christian faith in action.

The Korean ambassador to the United States, Chan Yang, invited Bob Lunney to accept the medal and citation on behalf of his fellow officers and the rest of the ship's crew. He did so, receiving the recognition from the Korean Consul General, D. Y. Namkoong, in New York on June 3, 1958.

The ship herself was retired to the Navy's "mothball fleet" after the Korean War but was pressed into service again in 1966, along with 160 other cargo ships from the reserve fleets, after the tense situation in Vietnam exploded into a full-scale war. A news release from the Commerce Department on October 30 of that year said the *Meredith Victory's* recall to active duty "is a case of a veteran returning to the wars, again to aid an Asian nation in its fight against Communism to maintain its independence."

The news release also pointed to the irony involving the ship. "Among the allies to whom it will carry supplies in Southeast Asia," the Commerce Department said, "will be thousands of South Korean troops who may well remember that it was this ship that saved 14,000 of their own people from extermination when they, too, fought for freedom from Communism. It may well be that some will remember the name of this ship, for the government of South Korea gave recognition to the exploits of the ship and its crew."

The ceremonies in which the *Meredith Victory* was returned to war duty also enabled the United States government to make good on an honor six years overdue. Shortly after being designated as a Gallant Ship in 1960, she was retired to the mothball fleet, before the bronze plaque signifying her designation could be completed and mounted on the ship. Presenting the plaque as a part of her recommissioning ceremonies filled that void.

Senator Warren G. Magnuson of Washington State, chairman of the Senate Commerce Committee, presented the new master and crew of the ship with the plaque, which the news release said was for "achieving the greatest rescue by a single ship in the annals of the sea." The plaque had gathered dust in the Commerce Building in Washington since 1960 while the ship herself lay in the Maritime Administration's National Defense Reserve Fleet in Olympia, Washington.

This time the man who had been the ship's captain in 1950, Brother Marinus, did not make the trip. He remained in the monastery in New Jersey, living the contemplative life of his calling, but took time to write a letter to those participating in ceremonies honoring the ship again. In his letter, Brother Marinus wrote:

> During the Korean War, I enjoyed the privilege of sailing in this vessel. At present, and for the past twelve years, I have been holding down a berth in another vessel, namely the barque [a small boat] of Peter. Though approximately sixty miles separate the monastery from the sea (jokingly, we say the beach is a little wider here), the news of the reactivation rekindles a host of vibrant and treasured memories of a gallant ship and her complement utilized in a gallant mission of mercy and justice. Distance cannot separate us from cherished recollections of the *Meredith Victory* and the men who constituted her complement.
>
> Once again, in a national crisis, the *Meredith Victory* will be engaged in an effort to help stem the scourge and evil of communist aggression. May she and all who serve on her be successful in this endeavor!
>
> Please convey to the master, officers, and seamen of the *Meredith Victory* my sincere congratulations in their new assignment. May they always uphold the highest traditions and ideals of our country and our Merchant Marine. Wishing them God speed and all blessing, sincerely in Christ—Brother Marinus, O.S.B., Ex-Master, SS *Meredith Victory*.

In 1993, the *Meredith Victory*'s storied life came to an inglorious end. Her "Vessel Status Card" on file at the United States

Maritime Administration in Washington traces her entire lifetime beginning with her delivery to Los Angeles at 2:20 P.M. Pacific War Time on July 24, 1945, with three weeks left in World War II. The final entry on her card says, in capital letters, "SOLD FOR SCRAP TO NISHANT IMPORT/EXPORT CO., LONDON— 10/01/93," a common ending for such an uncommon vessel. In a touch of irony, the scrapping reportedly took place in China, with the Chinese finally able to destroy the ship that boldly defied their efforts forty-three years before, with no protection and without firing a shot of her own.

Her story is preserved, however, in the Gallant Ship Room at the American Merchant Marine Museum at the Merchant Marine Academy on Long Island, New York. A plaque on the south wall dominates the room. It says:

> At the height of the epoch-making evacuation of Hungnam, Korea, by the United Nations Forces in December 1950, the SS *Meredith Victory* was requested to assist in the removal of Korean civilians trapped and threatened with death by the encircling enemy armies. Most of the military personnel had been pulled out and the city was aflame from enemy gunfire. Despite imminent danger of artillery and air attack and while her escape route became more precarious by the hour, the *Meredith Victory*, her tanks full of jet fuel, held her position in the shell-torn harbor until 14,000 men, women, and children had crowded into the ship. One of the last ships to leave Hungnam, the *Meredith Victory* set her course through enemy minefields and although having little food and water and neither doctors nor interpreters accomplished the three-day voyage to safety at Pusan with her human cargo including several babies born en route without a single loss of life. The courage, resourcefulness, sound seamanship, and teamwork of

her master, officers, and crew in successfully completing one of the greatest marine rescues in the history of the world have caused the name of the ship
the *Meredith Victory* to be perpetuated as that of a
gallant ship.

CLARENCE G. MORSE   FREDERICK H. MUELLER
Maritime Administrator   Secretary of Commerce

Did General Haig's career since Korea, especially his service as
secretary of state and the luxury of 20/20 vision that comes with
hindsight, ever prompt him to question whether the United
States should ever have become involved in the Korean War?
Was it worth it?

He answered immediately and emphatically, "Yes, absolutely. It
was at a very crucial time in the Cold War. I've been a little critical of Truman, but in the final analysis, whether it was Turkey
or Greece or Korea, he was a gutsy leader who understood the
broad strategic implications of this. We did the right thing."

What about the future?

"Whether Korea becomes united and free or the current stale-
mate continues into the indefinite future will depend on the
kind of American foreign policy that's conducted. And that
means a number of things. It means a realistic relationship
with the Chinese. It means a continuing bond of strategic part-
nership between Japan and the United States. And it means
understanding that you have to try to divine where the other
side is coming from. And sometimes that demands contact,
even though these are very tough, uncompromising people. It
also means you can't be naive, and there's been a high dosage
of naivete in this administration's policy toward the North, in
my view."

The Clinton administration is not the only target of criticism by General Haig on the subject of foreign policy. In looking back at the Korean War, the former secretary of state said, "I didn't think we conducted the war properly, but most importantly, we never understood the China dimension, just as we are failing to understand it today in my own party. We have these Republican Congressmen who can't get us in a war fast enough. And, of course, they'll be gone when the shooting starts."

Besides, he said, China doesn't want a war with the United States anyhow. "The Chinese don't want to have trouble with us," he said. "They want our moxie and our economic know-how."

Others share Haig's conviction that the Korean War was worth it. One Army veteran from Hungnam, Fred Long of the Third Infantry Division, told me, "Yes, the war was necessary. As with all human endeavor, the only final way to show resolve in protecting your way of life is to be willing to fight for it. Demonstrating willingness in Korea (and yes, even in Vietnam) deterred the big enemy—the Soviet Union—to the point where they quit."

President Truman said somewhat the same thing about stopping the Russians in Korea, then added a telling comment about the involvement of the United Nations in the war. In Merle Miller's 1973 oral biography of Truman, the president said the decision to fight against the North Koreans with an *international* force was a key distinction between the Korean War and the one in Vietnam, where American involvement reached full-scale combat involvement eleven years after the end of the shooting in Korea.

Truman told Miller, "For the first time in history, an aggressor was opposed by an international police force, and it worked. It saved the free world."

Dean Acheson agreed with the president. "When the Russians, to their great surprise, found that they had started something which the United States met absolutely squarely and hit with the utmost vigor," Acheson told Miller, "I think they stopped, looked, and listened. And the whole history of the world has since changed . . . We have not had to fight a third world war, which, as Mr. Truman has often said, would destroy us all. What we did in Korea, fighting a limited war for limited objectives, was not an easy thing for many people to understand. Nevertheless, it was what had to be done and what was done."

John Middlemas thinks Korea "was a war that should have been won. We didn't have the damn guts to go all the way. We should just have told the Chinese and the Koreans, 'You know, we have a couple of these bombs around . . . '" Even though the Soviet Union became an atomic power the year before starting the Korean War, Middlemas thinks we should have employed that strategy in our dealings with the Russians and the Chinese leaders.

"We don't know how to play chess," he said. Then he added, "We have people in government who are poor poker players."

At the same time, Middlemas harbors no ill will toward the Russian and Chinese people. "There were a lot of honorable people on the other side," he said. "They found themselves in that position, and they followed orders. Now can you condemn them for that forever? No. No. That's idiotic."

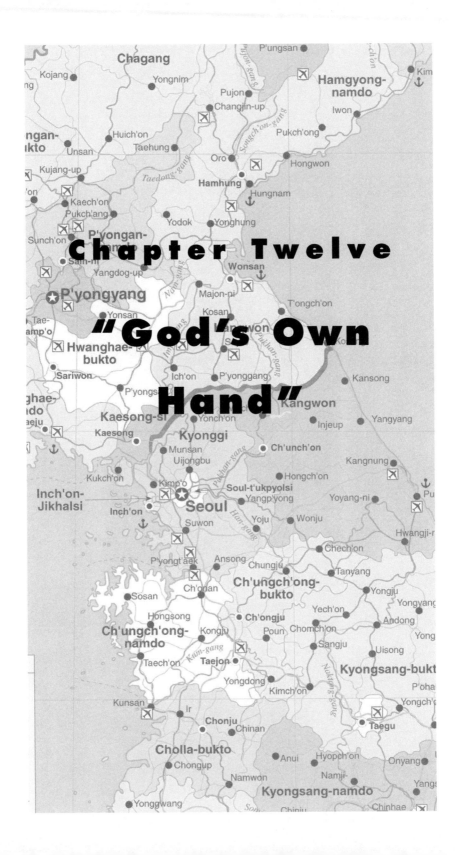

Chapter Twelve

"God's Own Hand"

In his article for *This Week* at Christmastime in 1958, Brother Marinus denied any connection between his experience in saving fourteen thousand refugees in 1950 and his entrance into the religious life four years later. "There were no bells ringing, and I was not knocked off a horse. It was just a culmination of things. It's what God wants me to do."

The sea captain turned monk elaborated, "I was always somewhat religious, even in my youth in Philadelphia. Man is composed of the sum total of his experiences, so all the things in my life helped to cement my determination to enter the monastery. However, I am certain that this one event . . . played a leading part in my decision."

That became clear when he also said, "I think often of that voyage. I think of how such a small vessel was able to hold so many persons and surmount endless perils without harm to a soul. And as I think, the clear, unmistakable message comes to me that on that Christmastide, in the bleak and bitter waters off the shores of Korea, God's own hand was at the helm of my ship."

Bibliography

Appleman, Lieutenant Colonel Roy E. *Escaping the Trap: The U.S. Army X Corps in Northeast Korea, 1950*. College Station, TX: Texas A&M Press, 1990.

Bajanov, Dr. Evgueni. "Assessing the Politics of the Korean War." Paper presented at a conference conducted by the Korea Society, Korea-America Society, and Georgetown University, Washington, DC, 1995.

Blair, Clay. *The Forgotten War*. New York: Times Books, 1992.

Bolin, Stanley F., Major John S. Cowings, and Kim Nam Che. *Twelve Hungnam Refugees*. Seoul: Headquarters, Eighth United States Army, 1975.

Dolcater, Captain Max W., Editor. *Third Infantry in Korea*. Tokyo: Third Infantry Division, 1953.

Dubuy, Lieutenant Colonel Carl T. "M*A*S*H: The Last Days at Hungnam, North Korea, with the First Mobile Army Surgical Hospital." Norfolk, VA: The General Douglas MacArthur Foundation, 1997.

Goulden, Joseph C. *Korea: The Untold Story of the War*. New York: Times Books, 1982.

Haig, Alexander M. Jr., and Charles McCarry. *Inner Circles: How America Changed the World: A Memoir*. New York: Warner Books, 1992.

Hakjoon, Dr. Kim. "Russian Foreign Ministry Documents on the Origins of the Korean War." Paper presented at a conference conducted by the Korean Society, Korea-America Society, and Georgetown University, Washington, DC, 1995.

Hastings, Max. *The Korean War*. New York: Simon and Schuster, 1987.

Hermes, Walter G. *Korean War*. Chicago: Worldbook-Childcraft International, Inc., 1978.

Hyun, Dr. Bong Hak, and Marian Hyun. "Christmas Cargo: A Civilian Account of the Hungnam Evacuation." Norfolk, VA: The General Douglas MacArthur Foundation, 1997.

Lawrence, Bill. *Six Presidents, Too Many Wars*. New York: Saturday Review Press, 1972.

Miller, Merle. *Plain Speaking: An Oral Biography of Harry S. Truman*. New York: Berkley Publishing Company, 1973.

Newsweek. "Korea: Can We Win the Political War, Too?" *Newsweek*, September 25, 1950.

Owen, Joseph R. *Colder than Hell*. Annapolis, MD: The Naval Institute, 1999.

Stanton, Shelby L. *America's Tenth Legion: X Corps in Korea*. Novato, CA: Presidio Press, 1989.

Summers, Harry G. Jr. *Korean War Almanac*. New York: Facts on File, 1990.

U.S. News & World Report. "40 Years After Korea—The Forgotten Story." *U.S. News & World Report, Inc.*, June 25, 1990.

Index